ZAKYNTHOS TRAVEL GUIDE 2025

The Ultimate Travel Companion to Greece's Emerald Island

ORLA WYN

Copyright © Orla Wyn 2025 All rights reserved. No part of this book may be reproduced, stored in a retrieval system, or transmitted in any form or by any means electronic, mechanical, photocopying, recording, or otherwise without prior written permission of the publisher, except for brief quotations used in reviews or scholarly works.

The information in this book is correct to the best of the author's knowledge at the time of publication. The author and publisher are not responsible for any errors, omissions, or changes in the content that may occur after the publication date

Table Of Contents

Welcome to Zakynthos...8
    Why Visit Zakynthos?.. 9
    Quick Facts & Geography... 10
    History in Brief... 11
    Local Culture and Traditions... 12

Planning Your Trip..13
    Best Time to Visit Zakynthos.. 13
    How to Get There (Flights & Ferries)................................... 14
    Getting Around Zakynthos... 15
    Language Tips & Greek Phrases.. 16
    Currency, Costs, and Budgeting... 17
    Travel Insurance and Safety Tips..19
    Internet, SIM Cards & Connectivity.....................................20
    Local Etiquette & Responsible Tourism...............................21

Top Must-See Attractions in Zakynthos............................... 22

Iconic Landmarks... 22
    Navagio Beach (Shipwreck Beach)...................................... 22
    Navagio Viewpoint (Above the Cliffs)..................................24
    Blue Caves (Agios Nikolaos).. 25
    Keri Lighthouse & Sunset Point... 28
    Bochali Hill and Venetian Castle..29
    Cameo Island (Agios Sostis)... 30

Stunning Beaches...32
    Gerakas Beach.. 32
    Porto Limnionas..34
    Xigia Sulfur Beach.. 36
    Banana Beach.. 37

Alykes & Alykanas Beaches.. 38
Kalamaki Beach..40
Dafni Beach... 41
Tsilivi Beach.. 42
Laganas Beach (Beach Bars & Nightlife)...................................... 43
Traditional Villages.. 44
Volimes Village (Local Products & Handicrafts)......................... 44
Keri Village..45
Agios Leon...46
Maries Village..48
Katastari...49
Anafonitria...51
Religious & Historical Sites.. 52
Anafonitria Monastery...52
Church of Agios Dionysios (in Zakynthos Town)........................53
St. Nicholas Church (on the Water)..55
Monastery of Skopiotissa... 56
Byzantine Museum of Zakynthos...57
Solomos Square & Statue...59
Natural Wonders.. 60
Keri Caves (Accessible by Boat or Kayak)..................................60
Marathonisi Island (Turtle Island)..62
Mizithres Rocks and Sea Views... 63
Askos Stone Park...65
Korakonissi Cove...66
Olive Groves & Zakynthian Countryside.................................... 67
Best Things to Do in Zakynthos... 69
Adventure & Outdoor Activities..69

    Snorkeling & Scuba Diving..70
    Sea Kayaking..71
    Hiking Trails (e.g., Skopos Mountain)...73
    Jeep Safari Tours..74
    Horseback Riding on the Beach..76
    Boat Tours Around the Island...77
    Sunset Cruises..79
    Paragliding at Kalamaki..80
Turtle Spotting Experiences...81
    Caretta Caretta Turtle Watching Tours...82
    Eco-friendly Turtle Conservation Tours...83
Family-Friendly Activities...85
    Water Village (Amusement Water Park)...85
    Fantasy Mini Golf..87
    Olive Oil Factory Tours...88
    Glass-Bottom Boat Tours..89
Cultural & Culinary Experiences...90
    Zakynthian Wine Tasting Tours..92
    Olive Oil and Honey Tasting...93
    Traditional Cooking Classes..95
    Folk Music & Dance Nights..96
    Local Markets & Artisan Shopping...97
Zakynthos Town (Zante Town)..99
    Strolling the Seafront Promenade..100
    Shopping in Roma Street...101
    Solomos & Kalvos Museum..103
    Church of Agios Dionysios..104
    Nightlife & Cafés...105

Hidden Gems in Zakynthos Town............ 107
Food & Drink in Zakynthos...................................... 108
　Must-Try Zakynthian Dishes................... 108
　Best Tavernas & Seafront Dining in Zakynthos........ 111
　Vegetarian & Vegan Options in Zakynthos.................114
　Beach Bars and Local Wines in Zakynthos............. 116
　Traditional Sweets & Desserts in Zakynthos..............119
Where to Stay in Zakynthos...................................... 122
　Best Areas to Stay.......................................122
　Top Resorts & Luxury Hotels................... 129
　Budget-Friendly Accommodations................. 130
　Family-Oriented Lodging........................ 132
　Romantic Getaways & Villas.........................135
　Agritourism & Village Stays..................... 136
Practical Travel Tips for Zakynthos.............................138
　Driving in Zakynthos (Rentals, Rules, Parking)..........138
　Emergency Contacts......................... 138
　Health & Medical Facilities........................ 139
　Accessibility Tips........................... 139
　Travel Apps & Tools for Zakynthos........................ 139
Glossary & Greek Phrases... 140
One More Look..142

Welcome to Zakynthos

I still remember the first time I set foot on Zakynthos. The scent of wild thyme and sea breeze filled the air as I stepped off the ferry, and the sun was setting over the Ionian Sea, casting a golden glow across the cliffs. It felt like the island was welcoming me with open arms. What started as a short escape turned into one of the most magical experiences of my life.

I wandered through quiet olive groves in Volimes, kayaked into glowing blue caves, watched loggerhead turtles glide beneath my boat in Laganas Bay, and stood breathless at the edge of the cliffs overlooking Navagio Beach the shipwreck far below like a secret from another world.

But it wasn't just the landscapes that stole my heart. It was the warmth of the people, the slow rhythm of island life, and the feeling that time didn't matter here.

This isn't just a guide, it's an invitation. I've gathered the soul of Zakynthos into these pages so you can feel the salt on your skin, the crunch of fresh olives, and the joy of watching a perfect sunset from a hidden cove. Whether you're looking for adventure, peace, or just a beautiful place to get lost in, you're about to explore it all.

Why Visit Zakynthos?

There's something quietly powerful about Zakynthos. It doesn't shout for attention, it simply waits for you to discover it. And when you do, it has a way of staying with you.

This island is known for its postcard-perfect sights, but it's so much more than that famous shipwreck beach. Yes, Navagio is breathtaking but so is the early morning stillness in a mountain village, the hush inside an old monastery, or the feeling of floating in a sea so clear you can see the sand ripple beneath you.

What makes Zakynthos special is its balance. You can spend one day exploring sea caves by boat, and the next lingering over grilled octopus and local wine at a quiet taverna. The island has hidden coves and cliffside views, but it also has friendly locals who will treat you like you've been coming there for years.

There's a rhythm to life here that pulls you in. Things slow down. The food tastes better. Even the air smells sweeter part salt, part pine, part something you can't quite name but won't forget. If you're drawn to places that feel real, places that still have their soul intact, Zakynthos is that kind of place. It's beautiful, yes, but more than that it's genuine. And that's what makes it worth the trip.

Quick Facts & Geography

Zakynthos, also called Zante by many, is one of the Ionian Islands off the western coast of Greece. It's the third largest in the group, and from the moment you arrive, it feels like the kind of place where the mountains meet the sea in the best possible way. The island covers just over 400 square kilometers, which makes it easy to explore by car or scooter without feeling rushed. To the west, you'll find rugged cliffs, sea caves, and wild, untouched coastlines. The east side has a little softer sandy beaches, lively resorts, and charming seaside towns. In the middle, rolling hills are dotted with olive groves, vineyards, and quiet villages where life moves at its own pace.

The capital, Zakynthos Town, sits on the east coast and is a good mix of history, culture, and local flavor. It's a great place to base yourself if you like to be near shops, harbor views, and restaurants. Just a short drive from town, you'll find peaceful countryside and views that make you want to pull over every five minutes.

History in Brief

Zakynthos has a long, layered history that you can actually feel when you're walking its streets or visiting its old churches. It's one of those places where the past hasn't been swept away, it's just quietly woven into daily life.

The island was named after Zakynthos, the son of a legendary Arcadian chief, and even gets a mention in Homer's *Iliad*. Over the centuries, it's seen a long parade of rulers: the Ancient Greeks, the Romans, the Byzantines, and later the Venetians, who left a deep mark on its culture and architecture. If you've ever wondered why some parts of Zakynthos feel more Italian than Greek, that's why.

The Venetians ruled for over 300 years and even nicknamed the island "Il Fiore di Levante" the Flower of the East because of its natural beauty. During that time, Zakynthos became known for its arts, literature, and music, which still play a big role in island culture today.

Later came brief occupations by the French and British, before Zakynthos finally united with the rest of Greece in the 19th century.

A huge turning point came in 1953, when a powerful earthquake hit the island and destroyed much of Zakynthos Town. Many historic buildings were lost, but the people rebuilt stronger, but without forgetting what came before.

Local Culture and Traditions

There's something beautifully genuine about the culture in Zakynthos. It's not put on for tourists, it's just part of daily life. People here are warm, expressive, and generous. Conversations don't happen in a hurry. Meals stretch on for hours. And there's always room at the table for one more.

Music plays a big role in Zakynthian life. The island has its own style of folk singing called *kantades*, a kind of romantic serenade that traces back to the Venetian era. You might hear it during a festival or even in a tucked-away taverna on a summer night, voices rising in harmony under the stars. Speaking of festivals Zakynthos loves them. Religious celebrations are big here, especially during Easter and on the feast day of Agios Dionysios, the island's patron saint. On those days, the streets fill with processions, music, flowers, and the scent of home-cooked food drifting from open windows.

Family is everything here. Traditions are passed down with care, and you'll see that in the way locals bake, celebrate, and speak with one another. Even something as simple as a glass of wine with friends feels like a small ritual.

Art, poetry, and theater have long been part of the island's identity, too. Locals take pride in their heritage, but they're also happy to share it without fuss, just with quiet confidence.

Planning Your Trip

Planning a trip to Zakynthos is part of the fun. It's the kind of place that doesn't require a rigid itinerary, just a bit of thought and a sense of adventure.

Best Time to Visit Zakynthos

Timing your trip to Zakynthos can really shape the kind of experience you'll have. The island changes with the seasons, and each one brings its own rhythm. If you're looking for that classic Greek summer vibe, long, sunny days, warm evenings, and a buzzing island full of life then June to early September is your window. This is peak season. The beaches are full, the tavernas are lively, and everything is open and running. It's perfect if you love the energy of summer and don't mind sharing the views.

For a more relaxed pace, late April to early June is a great choice. Spring hits early here, with wildflowers blooming along the cliffs and the sea beginning to warm up. You'll have space to breathe, the roads are quieter, and the air smells fresh and green. It's also when the island feels most "local."

September is a bit of a sweet spot. The weather's still warm, sometimes even hot but the crowds start to thin out. The sea is at its warmest after a whole summer of sunshine, and you'll find better prices on accommodation.

October slows things down even more. Some businesses begin to close for the season, but it's peaceful and still lovely for hiking, sightseeing, or simply doing nothing at all. Winter isn't a popular time to visit, and most tourist services shut down. But if you're just looking for quiet beauty and don't mind the cooler air, Zakynthos in the off-season has its own kind of charm.

How to Get There (Flights & Ferries)

Getting to Zakynthos is easier than you might expect for an island that still feels a bit off the beaten path.

If you're coming from abroad during the summer months, the quickest way is by plane. Zakynthos International Airport (ZTH) is small but well-connected. From May through October, there are direct flights from cities across Europe, especially the UK, Germany, Italy, and the Netherlands. If you're flying from outside Europe or during the quieter months, you'll likely connect through Athens.

From Athens, there are daily domestic flights to Zakynthos that take just under an hour. It's a smooth option if you want to skip the long drive and ferry. Now, if you like to travel at a slower pace and enjoy a bit of sea along the way, ferries are a solid option. From the mainland, you can catch a ferry from the port of Kyllini, which is about a 3.5-hour drive from Athens. The ferry ride to Zakynthos takes roughly an hour, and they run several times a day, especially in the high season. If you're renting a car, most ferries allow you to bring it along.

There's no ferry from Athens directly to Zakynthos, so Kyllini is your go-to port. During the summer, you'll also find some ferry routes connecting Zakynthos to nearby islands like Kefalonia, which is handy if you're doing a bit of island hopping.

Getting Around Zakynthos

Getting around Zakynthos really depends on how much of the island you want to see and how adventurous you're feeling.

The most popular and flexible option is renting a car. The island isn't huge, but the best spots like hidden beaches, mountain villages, or quiet viewpoints often aren't on main roads. With a car, you can explore at your own pace, stop for spontaneous photo breaks, and skip the crowds. Just keep in mind, some of the roads are narrow and winding, especially in the rural areas. Nothing too crazy, but it helps to be a confident driver.

If you're more of a two-wheels-and-the-wind kind of traveler, a scooter or quad bike is a fun alternative. They're great for short distances and zipping along the coast. Just make sure you're comfortable driving one, and always wear a helmet. The roads can be tricky in some places.

Public buses do exist, and they're fine if you're staying in more developed areas like Zakynthos Town, Laganas, or Tsilivi. Buses connect major towns and some beaches, but they don't run frequently and often stop early in the evening. They're cheap and reliable enough, but not ideal for deeper exploring.

Taxis are available, too, though they can be pricey if you plan to use them often. They're best for airport transfers or shorter rides when you don't feel like driving. In short, if you want freedom and a bit of adventure, get yourself a car or scooter. You'll see so much more of what makes this island special.

Language Tips & Greek Phrases

In Zakynthos, you'll find that many locals speak English, especially in the main towns and tourist areas. Still, tossing out a few Greek words here and there goes a long way. People genuinely appreciate the effort, and it's a great way to spark a smile or a bit of friendly conversation.

Greek might look intimidating at first with all those unfamiliar letters but you don't need to master the whole language to make a good impression. Just learning a handful of simple phrases can help you connect and show respect for the culture.

Here are a few helpful ones to keep in your pocket:

- **Kaliméra** (kah-lee-MEH-rah) – Good morning

- **Kalispéra** (kah-lees-PEH-rah) – Good evening

- **Efcharistó** (eff-kha-ree-STOH) – Thank you

- **Parakaló** (pah-rah-kah-LOH) – Please / You're welcome

- **Yásas** (YAH-sas) – Hello / Goodbye (formal or plural)

- **Ti káneis?** (tee KAH-nees) – How are you?

- **Nai** (neh) – Yes

- **Óchi** (OH-hee) – No

- **Signómi** (seeg-NO-mee) – Excuse me / Sorry

- **Poso kostízei?** (POH-so koh-STEE-zee) – How much does it cost?

Menus are often in both Greek and English, and signs around the island are usually easy to understand. Still, trying out a greeting or ordering in Greek can make everyday moments more fun. It's not about being perfect, it's about showing heart. And that's something locals always notice.

Currency, Costs, and Budgeting

Zakynthos uses the euro (€), just like the rest of Greece. ATMs are easy to find in towns and tourist areas, and most restaurants, hotels, and shops accept cards. Still, it's a good idea to carry some cash for small villages, beach tavernas, or family-run spots that prefer it.

As for how much you'll spend, Zakynthos can fit a range of budgets. You can travel here on a shoestring, go full luxury, or find a happy middle. It's up to you.

For a more budget-friendly trip, expect to spend around €50–€70 per day if you stay in a guesthouse, eat at local tavernas, and rent a scooter. Mid-range travelers might spend €100–€150 daily, with a rental car, a nice hotel or villa, and meals that include a few extras like fresh seafood or a sunset cocktail. If you're going for something upscale, with private tours, fine dining, and a beachfront suite, the sky's the limit.

Meals are usually of great value for the quality. You can enjoy a full Greek dinner with wine for under €20 per person at a local spot. Gyros and street snacks are even cheaper, perfect for days when you're on the go.

Car rentals range from €30–€60 per day in peak season. Tours (like boat trips to Shipwreck Beach or the Blue Caves) vary depending on group size and length, but are generally affordable.

Overall, Zakynthos is a place where you get a lot for what you spend, especially when it comes to views, food, and those small, unforgettable moments.

Travel Insurance and Safety Tips

Zakynthos is generally a very safe place to visit. The pace of life is relaxed, the locals are friendly, and crime is low. Still, it's always smart to be prepared just in case.

First things first: travel insurance. It's one of those things you hope you never need but will be so glad to have if something goes sideways. A good policy should cover medical emergencies, lost or stolen items, flight delays, and cancellations. It's especially important if you plan to rent a car, go boating, or do any adventurous activities like diving or hiking in remote areas.

Health-wise, the island has pharmacies and clinics in most towns, and there's a hospital in Zakynthos Town. For anything more serious, you may be transferred to a larger hospital on the mainland, so again insurance is a must.

As for staying safe day to day, a few simple habits go a long way. Don't leave valuables unattended on the beach or in your car. Keep your passport somewhere secure and carry a copy instead. If you're renting a scooter or quad bike, always wear a helmet and drive carefully. The roads can be narrow and winding. The sun can be deceptively strong, especially in July and August, so sunscreen, a hat, and staying hydrated are key. Also, if you're going for a swim at one of the wilder beaches or sea caves, check the currents and don't go too far from shore unless you're a confident swimmer.

Internet, SIM Cards & Connectivity

Staying connected in Zakynthos is pretty easy, and you won't have to go off the grid unless you want to.

Most hotels, guesthouses, cafes, and restaurants offer free Wi-Fi. It's usually good enough for emails, social media, and even video calls though in some remote or mountainous areas, the signal can be a bit patchy. If you're staying somewhere off the beaten path, it's worth asking about Wi-Fi quality when you book.

If you'd rather have internet access on the go, getting a local SIM card is a smart move. You'll find mobile shops in Zakynthos Town and in some of the larger resorts like Laganas or Tsilivi. Popular providers include Cosmote, Vodafone, and WIND. They offer tourist SIM packages with data, calls, and texts, and the setup process is usually quick and straightforward. Just bring your passport; they'll need it to register your SIM.

If your phone is unlocked, you're good to go. If not, check with your provider before you leave home. Some travelers also choose eSIM options, which can be activated instantly without swapping out your physical card super handy if your phone supports it.

Coverage across the island is generally solid, though some remote beaches and mountain roads might have weak signals. Still, you'll rarely be completely disconnected.

Local Etiquette & Responsible Tourism

Zakynthos may be a popular island for travelers, but it's also home to real communities, long-standing traditions, and a delicate environment that needs a little care and respect from everyone who visits.

The people here are warm, generous, and proud of their island. A simple "kaliméra" (good morning) or a friendly smile goes a long way. When visiting local villages or churches, it's polite to dress modestly, covering shoulders and avoiding beachwear in religious spaces shows respect. Greeks are also known for their hospitality, so if you're offered something, even just a glass of water, accepting it with a thank-you is a small but appreciated gesture.

Tipping isn't mandatory, but it's welcomed. Leaving a euro or two at a café, or rounding up the bill at a taverna, is standard. For tour guides, drivers, or housekeeping, a small tip is a nice way to show appreciation.

On the responsible tourism side, Zakynthos is especially sensitive because of its wildlife. This is one of the few places in the world where endangered loggerhead sea turtles (Caretta caretta) nest. If you're visiting their beaches, stick to marked paths, avoid disturbing the sand, and never touch the nests. Boat trips around turtle zones should keep a respectful distance if your captain doesn't, it's okay to speak up.

Top Must-See Attractions in Zakynthos

Zakynthos is packed with places that make you stop and stare sometimes out loud. The island may not be huge, but it's full of surprises, from iconic beaches to tucked-away villages. Here are the spots you really shouldn't miss.

ICONIC LANDMARKS

Zakynthos is bursting with unforgettable sights, and some spots simply can't be missed. These landmarks are the soul of the island, each one offering its own flavor of beauty, history, or jaw-dropping scenery. They're more than just great photo ops; they tell a story and give you moments that stay with you long after you've returned home.

Navagio Beach (Shipwreck Beach)

Navagio Beach isn't just famous, it's the kind of place that takes your breath away the moment you see it. Picture a remote cove enclosed by towering white cliffs, electric blue waters, and a rusty shipwreck resting on brilliant white pebbles. It's one of those rare places that looks even better than the postcards. Once you step onto the beach and feel the dramatic scenery wrap around you, you'll understand why it's often ranked among the most beautiful beaches in the world.

The beach gets its name from the MV Panagiotis, a smuggler's ship that ran aground during a storm in the 1980s. Its rusted skeleton still lies in the sand, giving the whole place a wild, mysterious feel. You won't find any sunbeds or cafés here, just nature at its most dramatic. The cliffs rise straight up from the beach, creating a secluded, awe-inspiring atmosphere that feels completely untouched.

You can't drive directly to Navagio Beach. It's only accessible by sea, which makes getting there part of the adventure. Boat tours run daily from several spots, including Porto Vromi, Agios Nikolaos, and Zakynthos Town.

Some are quick round-trips, while others include extra stops at sea caves and nearby beaches. Early morning trips are the most peaceful, while midday tends to be the busiest. Even though you can't stay long, boats usually give you an hour or so. It's more than enough time to walk the pebbles, snap some amazing photos, and take a swim in that surreal blue water. If you're a confident swimmer, you can even float out a little way to really take in the view of the cliffs and shipwreck from the sea.

Navagio Viewpoint (Above the Cliffs)

If seeing Navagio Beach from the shore feels like stepping into a dream, catching it from above is something else entirely. The viewpoint perched high above the cliffs offers one of the most jaw-dropping, camera-grabbing sights in all of Greece. Standing there, you're looking straight down into a cove so perfectly sculpted it seems like it can't be real: the dazzling turquoise water, the dramatic limestone walls, and the legendary shipwreck resting on the beach like a fossil from another time. It's a moment that makes your heart skip.

The viewpoint is located near the village of Anafonitria in the island's northwest corner. It takes about 45 minutes to drive from Zakynthos Town, and the route winds through scenic countryside and olive groves. The last stretch is narrow and a bit bumpy, but it's manageable and well worth the effort. Once you arrive, there's a small parking area near the official viewing platform.

The platform itself is safe and easy to access, offering a framed look at the beach below. But if you're after that dramatic cliff-edge photo that you see all over social media, there's a short, unofficial path off to the right of the platform. It leads to a rocky outcrop with an open, unobstructed view of the entire bay. It's a thrilling spot to stand but be cautious, as there are no barriers and the drop is sheer. The light is best early in the morning or late in the afternoon, when the sun isn't too harsh and the shadows bring depth to the cliffs.

If you're planning to visit by car, it's easy to pair this stop with a boat trip from nearby Porto Vromi or a visit to Anafonitria Monastery. You'll find a couple of snack stands and souvenir shops near the parking lot too, in case you want to grab a cold drink or pick up a keepsake.

Navagio Viewpoint is one of those places where silence seems to fall naturally. People tend to speak in hushed tones, stunned by the view. It's more than just a photo opportunity, it's a moment you'll remember every time someone asks you about your trip to Zakynthos.

Blue Caves (Agios Nikolaos)

The Blue Caves are one of Zakynthos' natural wonders, a mesmerizing network of sea-carved arches and chambers where light and water come together in the most magical way. Located near the port village of Agios Nikolaos on the island's northeast coast, these caves are famous for their dazzling shades of blue.

The reflections bounce off the white stone walls and turn the water into a glowing sapphire mirror. It's the kind of place that leaves you speechless, even if you've seen the photos before arriving.

The only way to reach the caves is by boat, and that's part of what makes the experience so special. From Agios Nikolaos, small boats depart throughout the day, offering guided tours that glide through the arches and along the sculpted coastline.

You can also find tours leaving from Makris Gialos or Skinari, and many of them pair the caves with a trip to Navagio Beach. For a more private adventure, there are smaller boats that carry just a handful of people, and even glass-bottom boats for a closer look at the underwater scene.

As your boat slips into the first of the caves, the color shift is immediate and stunning. Light filters in through the water and dances across the walls in every direction. Some caves are wide enough for the boat to enter completely, while others you float beside and admire from just outside. If your boat is small enough, you might get the chance to stop and swim, and there's nothing quite like diving into water so blue it almost looks unreal.

Early mornings are a fantastic time to go, when the sun hits the water at just the right angle and the area isn't crowded yet. The light becomes softer later in the day, giving the caves a moodier, more tranquil feel. Bring a waterproof camera or a dry bag. There are endless moments you'll want to capture, and it's easy to get splashed along the way.

Visiting the Blue Caves isn't just a sightseeing trip, it's an experience that stays with you. The colors, the light, the quiet rhythm of the waves against the stone... It's Zakynthos at its most beautiful and wild.

Keri Lighthouse & Sunset Point

Keri Lighthouse isn't just a place you visit, it's a feeling. It sits high above the Ionian Sea on the cliffs of the village of Keri, watching over the edge of the island like a quiet guardian. And when the sun starts its slow dip toward the horizon, this spot becomes something truly magical. The views are wide open and dramatic, the sea stretching endlessly in front of you, glowing gold and orange as the sky shifts through every shade. It's easily one of the most breathtaking sunset spots in all of Zakynthos.

The lighthouse itself is charming in its simplicity. It's not massive or flashy, but it fits the landscape perfectly, tucked into the rocky terrain with a kind of timeless grace. Around it, the cliffs fall steeply down to the sea, and if you take a short walk along the nearby trail, you'll find a few hidden viewpoints where the perspective becomes even more spectacular. The contrast between the rugged cliffs and the glowing water below is unforgettable.

To reach Keri Lighthouse, drive south from Zakynthos Town toward Keri village. The trip takes about 40 minutes, winding through olive groves, pine forests, and peaceful countryside. Once in Keri, follow the signs toward the lighthouse. There's parking nearby and a few tavernas perched right on the edge, where you can sip a drink or enjoy a local dish while the sky puts on its evening show.

Bochali Hill and Venetian Castle

Bochali Hill feels like Zakynthos' quiet little secret, sitting just above the bustling capital yet offering a peaceful escape with the kind of view that makes you stop mid-sentence. From up here, the town stretches out below in a patchwork of rooftops, the harbor curves around the sea, and the horizon seems endless. It's the perfect place to take a breath, soak it all in, and let the island reveal itself from a higher perspective.

Tucked among the pine trees on the hill is the Venetian Castle, a beautiful ruin that whispers stories of the island's past. Built during the 15th century when the Venetians ruled Zakynthos, the castle is a mix of crumbling stone walls, arched gateways, and overgrown courtyards.

It's not polished or overly restored, and that's what makes it so charming you can still feel the history in its weathered stones and quiet corners. Walk through its old bastions and you'll find shaded spots perfect for a peaceful pause and a glimpse of the sea through the trees.

Getting to Bochali Hill is quick and easy. It's just a five-minute drive from Zakynthos Town, or a 20-minute uphill walk if you're feeling adventurous. Once at the top, you'll find a few cozy cafes and benches where locals like to linger, especially around sunset. It's a lovely place to unwind after a day of sightseeing, especially with a cold drink in hand and a soft breeze carrying the scent of pine.

Cameo Island (Agios Sostis)

Cameo Island is the kind of place that makes you pause and smile the moment you see it. Tucked just off the southern coast of Zakynthos, near the village of Agios Sostis, this tiny, privately-owned island is like something from a postcard connected to the mainland by a charming wooden footbridge stretched over clear turquoise waters.

The moment you step onto that bridge, it feels like you're walking into a secret hideaway, far removed from the buzz of the mainland. The island itself is small but full of charm. White fabric flags flutter in the sea breeze, strung high above the shore like ribbons against the sky.

The beach here is compact, with soft pebbles and crystal-clear water that's perfect for a refreshing dip. It's a popular spot for couples, thanks to its dreamy views and romantic vibe, and it has even become a sought-after wedding venue in recent years. During the day, it's quiet and relaxed, and in the evenings, the place transforms with gentle lighting and music drifting across the water.

To get to Cameo Island, head to the southern village of Agios Sostis just a short drive from Laganas. There's parking nearby, and the entrance to the island is clearly marked. There's a small fee to cross the bridge, but it includes a drink ticket that you can use at the beach bar once you're on the island. It's open daily during the summer season, and it's best to arrive early if you're hoping to grab a spot on the beach or snap photos without a crowd.

This little slice of paradise is perfect for a short, scenic stop on your day's adventure. It's small, no doubt, but it has a special kind of magic that stays with you long after you leave. If you're looking to slow down and savor a peaceful moment in a truly picturesque spot, Cameo Island delivers it effortlessly.

STUNNING BEACHES

Zakynthos is one of those rare places where every beach feels like it could be the cover of a travel magazine. The island's coastline is incredibly diverse. One moment you're walking barefoot on soft golden sand, and the next you're climbing down a rocky path to find a hidden cove with turquoise water so clear you can count the pebbles at the bottom.

Gerakas Beach

Gerakas Beach is one of those rare places that stirs a sense of peace the moment your feet touch the sand. Tucked away on the southern tip of Zakynthos, its breathtakingly beautiful golden sands stretch into clear, shallow water that glows with soft blue and green hues. But it's more than just stunning. It's special. This beach is one of the most important nesting grounds for the endangered loggerhead sea turtles, or Caretta caretta, and that gives the place a quiet kind of magic. The beach is long and gently curved, backed by clay cliffs that glow in the afternoon light. There are no water sports or loud music here.

The atmosphere is calm, laid-back, and respectful. You'll find a few umbrellas and sunbeds, but much of the beach is left open to protect the turtle nests. In fact, certain areas are completely off-limits to visitors during nesting season, which runs from May to October, and you'll often see small enclosures around the turtle nests.

To get to Gerakas, head to the Vasilikos Peninsula. It's a straightforward drive from Zakynthos Town about 30 to 40 minutes depending on traffic and there's a small parking lot near the entrance. From there, it's a short walk down a wooden path through protected dunes and shrubs until the beach opens up in front of you.

Because it's part of the Zakynthos Marine Park, there are a few important rules in place to protect the turtles. You'll be asked not to bring large beach umbrellas, avoid digging in the sand, and leave just after sunset so the beach stays undisturbed for nesting.

Porto Limnionas

Porto Limnionas isn't your typical sandy beach, it's a rocky cove tucked into the west coast of Zakynthos, and it's absolutely breathtaking. When you first catch sight of it from above, the water looks almost unreal shades of sapphire and emerald shimmering between dramatic cliffs.

It's the kind of place that stops you in your tracks. The beauty here feels untouched, wild, and deeply refreshing. To reach Porto Limnionas, you'll need to drive through a scenic route across the island, heading toward the village of Agios Leon. The roads wind through olive groves and tiny mountain villages before you descend toward the coast. There's a parking area at the top, and from there, a short but slightly steep path leads down to the rocks.

What makes Porto Limnionas so unmissable is the swimming. The water is crystal clear, perfect for diving, snorkeling, or just floating lazily as the sun warms the rocks around you. You'll find underwater caves to explore, and if you're lucky, you might spot small fish darting beneath the surface. There's no sand here, so bring good water shoes or be ready to sunbathe on the smooth rocks.

There's a family-run taverna right by the cove with incredible views. Grab a bite to eat, sip something cold, and just take in the scene. It's easy to lose track of time. This spot feels like a well-kept secret, the kind of place you'll want to tell your friends about but also secretly keep to yourself. It's wild, rugged, and absolutely worth the journey.

Xigia Sulfur Beach

Xigia Sulfur Beach is unlike any other beach on Zakynthos. Tucked away on the island's northeast coast, it's small, quiet, and incredibly unique thanks to its natural sulfur springs that bubble up from the seabed. The moment you arrive, there's a faint but unmistakable scent in the air that's the sulfur and it's part of what makes this little cove so special. Locals often call it a natural spa, and after a swim, you'll understand why.

The water here has a milky, turquoise tint, especially where the sulfur mixes with the sea. It's said to have healing properties, great for your skin and joints, and even if you don't buy into the health claims, you'll still feel like you're bathing in something truly magical. The contrast between the bright blue sea and the steep limestone cliffs surrounding the beach is striking and gives the whole spot a peaceful, tucked-away vibe.

Getting to Xigia is easy if you're driving. Head north from Zakynthos Town or east from Alykes, and keep an eye out for the signs along the coastal road. There's parking above the beach and a steep path that takes you down to the pebbly shore. The descent is short but a bit uneven, so comfortable shoes help.

A few sunbeds and umbrellas are available, and there's usually a small canteen or a food truck above the beach where you can grab snacks and drinks. Some days, a pulley basket lowers cold refreshments straight down to you, a quirky little touch that fits the relaxed atmosphere of the place.

Banana Beach

Banana Beach is where Zakynthos turns up the energy. It's the longest beach on the island, and the moment your feet touch the soft golden sand, you'll feel like you've arrived at a sun-soaked playground. The beach stretches wide and far, with plenty of space to lounge, play, and soak up the Ionian sunshine. The water is a brilliant shade of blue, warm and shallow, perfect for swimming or just wading in with a cool drink in hand.

Getting to Banana Beach is straightforward. It's located on the southeast coast in the Vasilikos area, and it's well signposted from both Argassi and Zakynthos Town. There's a large parking area close to the beach, and many resorts in the area offer shuttle services.

Once you're there, everything is easy: sunbeds, umbrellas, beach bars, and even changing facilities are all within reach.

But it's not just a place to relax. Banana Beach is known for its vibrant vibe and water sports scene. You'll hear the hum of jet skis and laughter from people trying parasailing or being flung off banana boats. There's something happening all the time, and the upbeat atmosphere is contagious. Even if you're just lying on a lounger, the energy buzzes around you.

Several beach clubs line the shore, each with their own music, cocktails, and menus. You can spend the whole day here, grab lunch in your swimsuit, sip a frozen drink, then head back to the sea. As the afternoon rolls in, the light softens and the beach becomes even more photogenic. Banana Beach is fun, carefree, and full of life. It's exactly where you want to be when you're in the mood for a sunny, lively escape by the water.

Alykes & Alykanas Beaches

Alykes and Alykanas are two neighboring beaches on Zakynthos' northeast coast that offer a perfect blend of laid-back charm and family-friendly energy. These sandy stretches are ideal if you're looking for soft golden shores, calm shallow waters, and a touch of local village life. They're not flashy or overly touristy; they're welcoming, warm, and wonderfully relaxing.

Reaching them is easy, especially if you're staying in the nearby resorts or villages. Alykes is about a 25-minute drive from Zakynthos Town, and Alykanas sits just next door. You can even walk between the two along the beach if you feel like stretching your legs with a sea breeze at your side. Parking is usually available near the waterfront, and the roads leading in are smooth and straightforward. What makes these beaches stand out is the gentle sea, clear, calm, and shallow for quite a distance, making it ideal for families with children or anyone wanting a peaceful swim. You'll spot colorful little fishing boats bobbing in the water and maybe even a turtle or two during the quieter months. The sand is soft and spacious, great for sunbathing or long afternoon walks along the shore.

Both Alykes and Alykanas are lined with inviting tavernas and cafes where you can enjoy local dishes without stepping far from the water. Think grilled octopus, fresh village salad, and an ice-cold drink as you watch the waves roll in. If you're up for a little activity, there are water sports on offer too, nothing too wild, just enough to keep things fun and lively.

These beaches are the kind of place you end up staying longer than planned. The mix of natural beauty, calm waters, and the low-key buzz of village life gives Alykes and Alykanas a special rhythm. It's easy to fall into it and just let the day unfold at its own pace.

Kalamaki Beach

Kalamaki Beach is one of those places that instantly puts you at ease. Tucked along the southern coast of Zakynthos, it stretches out in a long, wide embrace of golden sand and gentle, clear waters. It's part of the protected National Marine Park, which means you won't find loud beach bars or jet skis here, just the soothing rhythm of waves and a peaceful atmosphere that feels miles away from the world.

Getting to Kalamaki is quick and simple. It's only about a 10-minute drive from Zakynthos Town and right next to Laganas, though it feels like a different world entirely. The beach is easily accessible by car or scooter, and there's usually convenient parking close by. A short walk from the main road through the village will lead you straight onto the sand. This beach is also famous for a truly heartwarming reason: it's a nesting site for the endangered loggerhead sea turtles. If you visit between June and August, you might spot marked nesting areas in the sand. These are protected zones where turtles have laid their eggs, and it's important to give them space. Sunrise and early morning walks often offer the best chance to see signs of these shy, ancient creatures.

Kalamaki is the kind of beach where time slows down. The water is shallow and perfect for swimming, and the backdrop of green hills adds to its charm. There are a few laid-back tavernas set just off the sand where you can sip something cool and enjoy the local flavors without ever needing to put your shoes back on.

Dafni Beach

Dafni Beach is a true hidden treasure on Zakynthos' southern coast. Tucked away in the Vasilikos Peninsula, this unspoiled stretch of coastline feels like a secret known only to those who make the effort to find it. The scenery here is simply breathtaking clear turquoise waters, soft golden sand, and a sweeping view of the Ionian Sea framed by rugged cliffs and olive groves.

To reach Dafni Beach, you'll need to take a winding, narrow road that descends from the main route connecting Vasilikos and Argassi. It's a bit of an adventure, but nothing too challenging if you're driving carefully. Once you reach the bottom, a small parking area awaits, and from there, you're just a few steps from the sand. The slightly off-the-beaten-path journey is more than worth it.

What makes Dafni truly special is its role as a protected nesting ground for loggerhead sea turtles. Like Kalamaki, this beach is part of the Zakynthos Marine Park, so you won't find jet skis or loud music here. Instead, there's a peaceful vibe that invites you to slow down and soak in the surroundings. You might even catch a glimpse of baby turtles making their way to the sea during hatching season. There are a couple of charming tavernas built right on the hillside, offering delicious fresh seafood and chilled drinks with panoramic views. You can spend hours swimming, sunbathing, and simply gazing out over the horizon.

Tsilivi Beach

Tsilivi Beach is one of Zakynthos' liveliest and most inviting coastal spots, perfect for travelers looking for a mix of fun, comfort, and natural beauty. Just a ten-minute drive north of Zakynthos Town, this beach is incredibly easy to reach and is well-connected by public buses and taxis. If you're staying in the area, many accommodations are just a short stroll away from the shoreline.

The beach itself stretches wide and long, with soft golden sand that's ideal for sunbathing and sandcastle-building. The shallow, crystal-clear waters are great for swimming and safe for kids, making it a family favorite. You'll also find plenty of sunbeds and umbrellas available for rent, so settling in for a day at the beach is as easy as it gets.

Tsilivi is also a hot spot for water sports. From banana boat rides to paddleboarding and jet skiing, there's no shortage of activity here. For those who prefer a more laid-back experience, the beachfront is lined with tavernas, bars, and cafés where you can sip a cold drink or enjoy fresh seafood with your toes still in the sand. As the day winds down, Tsilivi doesn't quiet down. The sunset views over the Ionian Sea are absolutely breathtaking, and when night falls, the beach area buzzes with music, lights, and a festive atmosphere. Tsilivi Beach isn't just a place to visit, it's a place to enjoy from sunrise to after dark, offering something for every kind of traveler.

Laganas Beach (Beach Bars & Nightlife)

Laganas Beach is where the sun meets the party. Located on the southern coast of Zakynthos, just a 15-minute drive from Zakynthos Town and a quick ride from the airport, this beach is famous for its wide stretch of golden sand and its electric energy that flows straight into the night. It's one of the most visited spots on the island, and once you feel the vibe, it's easy to see why.

By day, Laganas is a hotspot for lounging and swimming. The water is shallow and calm, perfect for long wades or simply cooling off under the Greek sun. Beach bars line the shore, each with its own flavor, some offering laid-back cocktails and sunbeds, others turning up the music early in the afternoon. Many places also serve food right to your lounge, so you never have to move far to keep your day going strong.

When the sun dips low, Laganas transform. The beach bars glow with lights, the music picks up, and the whole area comes alive. Clubs and lounges spill onto the sand, and the party continues well into the early hours. You'll find a mix of international DJs, live shows, and themed parties every night of the week during peak season. It's loud, lively, and full of energy, making it one of the island's most unmissable nightlife hubs. Despite its party reputation, Laganas is also known for its natural importance. The area is part of the National Marine Park, a protected nesting ground for loggerhead turtles.

TRADITIONAL VILLAGES

Zakynthos isn't just about beaches and nightlife; its soul is tucked away in the quiet charm of its traditional villages. These little pockets of local life offer a slower, more authentic pace where you can truly feel the island's heritage, taste homemade delicacies, and meet locals who still live much like their ancestors did. Wandering through these places is like stepping into living postcard stone houses, colorful courtyards, and the scent of olive trees in the breeze.

Volimes Village (Local Products & Handicrafts)

Volimes Village, nestled in the northern mountains of Zakynthos, is one of the most charming and authentic spots on the island. It's a place where tradition still runs strong and the slow rhythm of daily life gives you a welcome break from the busy coastline. The village itself is a postcard-perfect blend of stone houses, quiet streets, and stunning views of the surrounding hills and sea in the distance.

What really makes Volimes special is its reputation for local products and handicrafts. This is the heart of Zakynthian craftsmanship. As you walk through the village, you'll find small roadside stalls and family-run shops selling handmade lace, embroidered linens, beeswax candles, and pottery. These aren't factory-made souvenirs, they're pieces of heritage made by people who have been perfecting their work for decades.

Olive oil from the area is rich and golden, and the local honey, often infused with thyme or pine, is absolutely delicious. You'll also come across herbs, wines, and traditional sweets like mantolato and pasteli.

Getting to Volimes is straightforward. From Zakynthos Town, the drive takes about 40 to 45 minutes, winding through beautiful countryside and olive groves. It's also a convenient stop if you're heading to attractions like the Blue Caves or Navagio Viewpoint, as they're located in the same northern region. You'll want to have a car to get there, as public transport can be infrequent in the more rural parts of the island.

Keri Village

Keri Village is a hidden gem tucked into the lush hills of southwestern Zakynthos. With its winding cobbled paths, stone-built houses, and fragrant olive groves, it feels like stepping back into a quieter, simpler time. The village is traditional through and through, and that's exactly where its charm lies: nothing flashy, just a peaceful, authentic slice of island life.

As you stroll through Keri, you'll notice how warm and welcoming the atmosphere is. Locals chat over coffee in tiny cafés, cats nap in the shade, and colorful flowers spill from every windowsill. It's the perfect place to slow down, breathe deeply, and soak in the rich, rustic beauty around you.

The village is also known for its handcrafted goods, including lace and honey, sold in small family-run shops right off the main square. One of the biggest highlights near the village is the view from Keri Lighthouse, just a short drive away. From this dramatic clifftop, you'll get sweeping views of the Ionian Sea, especially magical at sunset. The cliffs drop steeply into the deep blue water, and on clear days, you can even spot the Mizithres rocks rising from the sea like ancient sentinels. It's a scene you'll carry in your memory long after you've left.

To get to Keri, you'll want to drive. It's about a 30-minute trip from Zakynthos Town and just under 20 minutes from Laganas. The roads twist and climb through olive groves and forests, offering glimpses of the coast along the way. While public buses do serve the area, they're not always reliable, so having your own transport will give you more freedom to explore.

Agios Leon

Agios Leon is one of Zakynthos' most authentic mountain villages, a peaceful retreat surrounded by wild nature, old-world charm, and traditions that haven't faded with time. Tucked away in the island's rugged interior, it's a place where you'll hear the quiet hum of bees in lavender fields, smell the scent of pine on the breeze, and see stone houses standing proud against a landscape of rolling hills.

The village is small but full of character. Its narrow streets lead you past ancient olive trees, hand-carved wooden doors, and tiny tavernas where local recipes have been passed down for generations. It's the kind of place that makes you want to stop for a long lunch, sip a glass of wine made just down the road, and chat with the friendly locals who always seem to have time for a story.

Agios Leon is also a hub for traditional products. Keep an eye out for roadside stalls selling homemade olive oil, wine, honey, and herbs picked from nearby hillsides. Everything here is produced with care and pride, and picking up a bottle of their extra-virgin olive oil or a jar of mountain honey makes for a meaningful souvenir you can actually taste. From the village, you can also venture out to some of the island's more off-the-beaten-path beaches. Porto Roxa and Porto Limnionas are both a short drive away and are known for their dazzling turquoise water and dramatic cliffs perfect spots for a refreshing swim and a lazy sun-soaked afternoon.

To get to Agios Leon, you'll need a car. It's about a 40-minute drive from Zakynthos Town through a scenic route filled with olive groves and winding hills. The journey is part of the experience, with views opening up to the sea as you climb higher into the countryside. Agios Leon offers a taste of real Zakynthos calm, beautiful, and steeped in tradition. It's not built for crowds or fast-paced sightseeing, but that's exactly what makes it unforgettable. Spend time here, and you'll feel like you've stumbled upon a secret that few travelers ever really find.

Maries Village

Maries Village is one of Zakynthos' hidden gems, a place that feels like it's been quietly waiting for curious visitors to discover its charm. Nestled in the hills on the western side of the island, this tiny mountain village is full of rustic beauty, history, and tranquility that offers a lovely contrast to the busier beach towns.

As you wander through Maries, you'll notice the simplicity of village life. Stone cottages with colorful shutters line the narrow lanes, and the scent of wild herbs drifts through the air. Locals here are warm and welcoming, and it's not unusual to find someone offering you a taste of their homemade honey or inviting you to sit under a shaded tree for a chat. The pace is slow in the best possible way. This is a place where time seems to stretch, letting you really take in every detail.

One of the village's most fascinating spots is the Church of Mary Magdalene. Legend has it that she visited the area during her travels, and a small monastery was later built to honor her. It's a peaceful, spiritual place that adds a special sense of depth to the village. Nearby, you'll also find local shops selling handcrafted soaps, olive oil, and delicate embroidery all made right here in the mountains by people who still work with tradition at heart.

Maries also acts as a fantastic base if you're heading to some of the island's wild western cliffs. The iconic view of Shipwreck Beach from the cliffs above is just a short drive away, and Porto Vromi is the nearest port if you're planning a boat tour to the Blue Caves or the famous shipwreck cove itself.

To reach Maries, it's best to rent a car. From Zakynthos Town, it's about a 45-minute scenic drive through winding roads and forested hills. The route is beautiful in its own right, with chances to stop and snap photos of the countryside along the way.

Katastari

Katastari is one of Zakynthos' largest villages and offers a refreshing blend of traditional character and everyday island life. Sitting quietly above the seaside town of Alykes on the island's northeastern coast, Katastari feels authentically Greek, with a lived-in charm and sweeping views over the Ionian Sea.

Walking through the village, you'll notice how life moves at a calm, steady pace. Locals gather in family-run cafes, chatting over coffee as the sun filters through olive trees. The buildings here range from classic stone homes to more modern dwellings, reflecting the village's natural evolution over the years while still holding tightly to its roots.

Katastari is a wonderful place to stop if you enjoy exploring without the usual tourist crowds. Small shops sell homemade olive oil, locally grown produce, and fresh bread still warm from village ovens. There's also a strong sense of community pride: gardens are neatly kept, and historic chapels and churches are lovingly preserved, with some offering quiet spots to rest and take in the peaceful surroundings.

One of the best things about Katastari is its elevated position. From certain points in the village, the view down to Alykes Beach and the bright blue stretch of sea beyond is simply breathtaking. On clear days, you can even spot the faint outline of Kefalonia across the water. It's a perfect place to stop and breathe in the island's beauty away from the bustle.

Reaching Katastari is easy by car. From Zakynthos Town, it's a 25-minute drive through olive groves and rolling hills. If you're staying near Alykes or Alykanas, it's just a few minutes uphill, making it an easy detour for an afternoon stroll or a sunset coffee with a view.

Katastari may not make every travel brochure, but it offers something just as valuable: a genuine connection to the island's culture and daily life. It's charming, relaxed, and full of little moments that stay with you long after you've left.

Anafonitria

Anafonitria is a timeless village tucked away in the lush hills of northwestern Zakynthos, and stepping into it feels like walking into a postcard from the past. This little corner of the island is wrapped in tradition, spirituality, and scenic beauty. It's peaceful, authentic, and surrounded by olive groves and vineyards that seem to stretch endlessly across the countryside.

The village is best known for the historic Anafonitria Monastery, a spiritual landmark that dates back to the 15th century. This is where Saint Dionysios, the island's patron saint, spent part of his life. The monastery still welcomes visitors with its stone walls, vine-covered courtyard, and quiet, contemplative atmosphere. Inside, you'll find stunning frescoes and religious icons that have been preserved for centuries, offering a powerful glimpse into the island's deep Orthodox roots.

Anafonitria isn't just about the monastery, though. The village itself has a quiet charm, with traditional stone houses and friendly locals who often sell homemade honey, herbs, and handwoven goods at roadside stalls. You'll likely smell the scent of thyme and oregano in the air as you wander the narrow lanes. It's an ideal spot for a relaxed walk, with moments of beauty around every turn. Getting to Anafonitria is simple by car. From Zakynthos Town, it takes about 40 minutes heading northwest, passing through scenic landscapes along the way. If you're visiting the famous Navagio Beach Viewpoint nearby, it's easy to include a stop in Anafonitria either before or after.

RELIGIOUS & HISTORICAL SITES

Zakynthos has a deep sense of history and faith that's woven into its landscapes, and exploring the island's religious and historical sites is like flipping through the pages of a living storybook. These places aren't just beautiful, they hold the spirit of the island, its resilience, and its deep-rooted traditions.

Anafonitria Monastery

Tucked away in the peaceful hills of northwestern Zakynthos, Anafonitria Monastery is one of the island's most treasured spiritual landmarks. Stepping into its stone courtyard feels like you've entered a hidden corner of history, where time slows down and every stone whispers stories of devotion. This is the place where Saint Dionysios, the patron saint of Zakynthos, spent part of his life in quiet reflection, and that sense of calm still lingers in the air.

The monastery dates back to the 15th century and carries the elegance of true simplicity. Don't expect flashy decorations, what makes Anafonitria so striking is its rugged charm and deeply spiritual atmosphere. Its thick stone walls, small arched windows, and faded frescoes speak volumes. Inside the church, flickering candles light up delicate icons, and the scent of old wood and incense lingers in the stillness. It's a beautiful, grounding experience.

Getting to Anafonitria Monastery is an easy drive from the popular areas of Zakynthos Town or Laganas. You'll head toward the northern part of the island, passing olive groves, vineyards, and sleepy villages. It's located near the village of Anafonitria, just a short distance from the famous Navagio Viewpoint, so it fits perfectly into a day exploring the island's rugged north.

Once there, take time to wander the grounds and soak in the views of the surrounding hills. There's a quiet dignity in the way the building stands, as if it's been patiently watching the landscape for centuries. Even if you're not particularly religious, this is a place that makes you pause and breathe a little deeper. It's not just a stop on a sightseeing list, it's a chance to feel something ancient and true. Anafonitria Monastery may not be flashy, but it's unmissable for travelers who want to see the soul of Zakynthos. It's a reminder that some of the island's most meaningful experiences don't come with beach umbrellas or boat rides; they come with silence, stone walls, and a sense of timelessness you can't quite explain.

Church of Agios Dionysios (in Zakynthos Town)

Standing proudly along the waterfront of Zakynthos Town, the Church of Agios Dionysios is far more than just an architectural gem; it's the spiritual heartbeat of the island. With its soaring bell tower and stately façade, this breathtaking church immediately grabs your attention. But it's what lies inside that truly leaves a lasting impression.

This sacred site houses the relics of Saint Dionysios, the island's beloved patron saint, and is a deeply meaningful place for locals and visitors alike. As you step through its doors, the hush of reverence is almost tangible. The interior is grand and ornate, yet warmly welcoming. Gilded chandeliers dangle from high ceilings, and every corner glows with the light of flickering candles. Vibrant frescoes, intricate icons, and a marble iconostasis stretch before you, drawing your eyes to the lavish altar. The scent of incense weaves through the cool air, grounding you in the moment. It's not just beautiful, it's moving.

The church is easily accessible, located on the southern edge of Zakynthos Town, right along the harbor promenade. You can walk to it from the town square in under ten minutes. Whether you're arriving by foot, taxi, or bus, you can't miss its towering bell tower, one of the tallest and most iconic landmarks on the island. It stands as a guiding light, both literally and symbolically.

The real heart of this church is the silver casket that holds the relics of Saint Dionysios. On special feast days particularly August 24 and December 17 the casket is paraded through the streets in a powerful, emotional procession. Even outside of these celebrations, visitors can view the casket behind glass and witness firsthand the devotion of those who come to pay their respects. The Church of Agios Dionysios is not just for those drawn to religious history. It's a captivating mix of cultural heritage, artistic craftsmanship, and island pride.

St. Nicholas Church (on the Water)

St. Nicholas Church, known locally as Agios Nikolaos tou Molou, is one of Zakynthos Town's most picturesque and charming landmarks. Perched right at the edge of the old port, it almost seems to float on the sea, giving it the nickname "on the water." The setting is downright breathtaking, with gentle waves lapping against its stone base and fishing boats bobbing nearby. It's the kind of place that quietly steals your heart without needing to try too hard.

Built in the 16th century, this is the oldest surviving Venetian church in Zakynthos Town. What makes it especially unique is its blend of architectural styles, classic Venetian lines mixed with traditional Greek touches. The stone walls and modest bell tower have a weathered beauty that speaks to centuries of storms, prayers, and change. Inside, things stay simple and soulful. The icon of Saint Nicholas, the patron saint of sailors, takes pride of place, and locals still stop in for a moment of quiet before heading out to sea.

Getting here is easy. The church is located at the edge of Solomos Square, the heart of Zakynthos Town. You can reach it on foot in just a few minutes from most central locations. As you stroll along the harborfront, the sight of the church jutting out into the water draws you in like a postcard come to life. It's a lovely detour on any walk through town, especially during golden hour, when the sun turns the sea and stone a glowing shade of amber.

Though small in size, St. Nicholas Church carries the weight of history with grace. It survived the devastating 1953 earthquake that destroyed much of the town, standing tall while many buildings crumbled. Today, that quiet resilience adds depth to its beauty. Spend a few peaceful minutes here, let the sea breeze wash over you, and listen to the gentle rhythm of the harbor. It's a moment of calm that stays with you long after you leave.

Monastery of Skopiotissa

High on Mount Skopos, tucked away from the usual buzz of Zakynthos, lies the Monastery of Skopiotissa, a peaceful, windswept gem with views that feel like a reward for the journey. This is the oldest monastery on the island, dating back to the 15th century, and it's perched at such a height that you can see across Zakynthos, the Ionian Sea, and even over to the Peloponnese on a clear day. The setting is so breathtakingly quiet that the only sounds you're likely to hear are chirping birds, rustling olive trees, and the whisper of the breeze.

The church at the heart of the monastery is dedicated to the Virgin Mary and has an elegant simplicity that fits perfectly with its remote location. Its whitewashed walls, worn stone floor, and old frescoes create an atmosphere of timelessness. There's a sense of history in every corner, from the weathered icons to the little arched doorways. It's not flashy or grand, but it radiates character and charm. And just outside, the courtyard opens up to a panoramic sweep of nature that's hard to describe without actually standing there.

Getting to the Monastery of Skopiotissa is part of the adventure. It's located above the village of Argassi, and the drive takes you partway up Mount Skopos. From there, you'll need to hike the final stretch. The trail is rocky but manageable, and the views just keep getting better the higher you climb. If you're visiting in the spring, the hillsides are carpeted in wildflowers, which makes the walk feel like a dream.

This spot is rarely crowded, which adds to its magic. It's a perfect escape if you're looking for something that feels deeply personal and completely different from the beach scene. Bring water, wear good shoes, and give yourself time to just sit and take it all in. The Monastery of Skopiotissa offers more than just a historic site; it gives you space to breathe, to look out over the world, and to feel a little awe.

Byzantine Museum of Zakynthos

Right in the heart of Zakynthos Town, facing the vibrant Solomos Square, the Byzantine Museum of Zakynthos stands as a beautiful surprise for anyone curious about the island's artistic soul. From the outside, its elegant facade is stately but modest, which makes stepping inside feel like opening a treasure chest. This museum is a quiet powerhouse of history, packed with rare icons, intricate frescoes, and religious art that survived the devastating 1953 earthquake.

As you walk through the spacious galleries, you'll find yourself face-to-face with vivid works from the 15th to 18th centuries, many salvaged from ruined churches and monasteries across the island. These pieces are far from dusty relics. They are bold, colorful, and full of personality. The wooden icon screens, in particular, are stunning. You'll find scenes bursting with emotion and detail, showcasing saints, biblical stories, and the unmistakable style of the Heptanese School that blended Byzantine tradition with Western flair.

The museum also does a beautiful job recreating the interiors of old churches that were destroyed, giving you a real feel for what Zakynthos' sacred spaces once looked like. There's a special hush in those rooms, as if time has pressed pause for a moment. And upstairs, there's a collection of sculptures and manuscripts that deepen the story even further. Everything is clearly labeled in English and Greek, which makes exploring the museum at your own pace easy and enjoyable.

Getting to the Byzantine Museum is simple. It's located right on the main square in Zakynthos Town, an easy walk from anywhere in the town center. If you're coming from other parts of the island, parking nearby is possible, though it's best to go early in the day when things are quieter. The museum is open most days, and the entry fee is modest, well worth it for the richness inside.

Solomos Square & Statue

Right at the beating heart of Zakynthos Town lies Solomos Square, a graceful open space that somehow manages to be both lively and relaxing at once. Surrounded by neoclassical buildings and kissed by sea breezes from the nearby harbor, this square is one of the island's most iconic gathering places. It's where history, culture, and everyday life gently collide and it's the perfect spot to pause and take it all in.

The focal point here is the statue of Dionysios Solomos, the island's most celebrated poet and the man behind Greece's national anthem. There's something powerful about standing in front of his statue, set against the wide blue backdrop of the Ionian Sea. You can't help but feel a spark of pride even if you're just visiting. The statue is more than just a tribute; it's a reminder of Zakynthos' deep contribution to Greek identity and literature.

All around the square, there's plenty to see and enjoy. The Zakynthos Public Library and the Byzantine Museum both face the square, so culture is literally at your fingertips. The wide marble-paved plaza is also great for people-watching. Locals stroll through with their coffee, kids ride their bikes in the open space, and visitors snap photos of the grand architecture that frames the scene. It all feels charming and alive, without being chaotic.

Getting to Solomos Square is incredibly easy. It's located right in the center of Zakynthos Town, just a short walk from the port. If you're driving, there are public parking areas nearby, though the square itself is pedestrian-only, which adds to its peaceful feel. In the evenings, the whole area glows with soft light and becomes a lovely place to wander after dinner or grab a drink at one of the nearby cafés.

Solomos Square is more than just a scenic stop, it's a place that tells a story. It captures the spirit of Zakynthos: proud, poetic, and open to everyone.

NATURAL WONDERS

Zakynthos is far more than just a beach destination. It's an island shaped by time, sea, and volcanic energy, a place where nature doesn't just quietly sit in the background but steals the show in dramatic, unforgettable ways. Its natural wonders are a huge part of what makes the island feel so alive, so raw, and so beautifully unpredictable.

Keri Caves (Accessible by Boat or Kayak)

Tucked along Zakynthos' rugged southwest coast, the Keri Caves are a breathtaking slice of natural beauty just waiting to be explored. These sea-carved grottos, framed by towering white cliffs and lapped by impossibly clear water, are some of the island's most magical places.

Light dances across the stone walls and creates dazzling reflections in the water. It's the kind of place that feels straight out of a fantasy film.

The only way to reach the caves is by sea, which adds a sense of adventure to the whole experience. You can book a boat trip from Limni Keri village, a quiet and charming spot that sits right on the edge of the bay. There are plenty of local operators offering guided tours, or if you're feeling a bit more adventurous, you can rent a kayak and paddle there yourself. The coastline is calm and scenic, with every turn offering fresh views of cliffs, secret coves, and patches of deep blue water.

Once you reach the caves, the real thrill begins. Boats can glide right inside the larger ones, and you'll find yourself floating through tunnels of shimmering blue and green light. Some caves are large enough to swim into, and others are more narrow and mysterious, perfect for a bit of exploring. If the sun's high in the sky, the water becomes so clear that you can see straight down to the seabed. It's like snorkeling in glass.

Don't forget your camera, but be warned no photo will ever do the place justice. The colors, the silence, the echo of water against stone it's something you need to feel for yourself. And if you go by kayak, you'll have the added bonus of setting your own pace, stopping along the cliffs to swim or rest whenever you like.

The Keri Caves offer a quieter, more intimate experience compared to some of Zakynthos' more famous sights. They're not crowded or commercialized, just wild, beautiful, and unspoiled. It's the kind of trip that stays with you, long after your skin dries off and your clothes stop smelling of saltwater. If you're looking to connect with the island's raw beauty, this is an unmissable stop.

Marathonisi Island (Turtle Island)

Marathonisi Island, often called Turtle Island, feels like a dreamy escape floating in the heart of Laganas Bay. With its soft, pale sands and untouched natural charm, this tiny islet is shaped like a turtle, a delightful nod to the endangered loggerhead sea turtles that use it as a nesting ground. The moment you see it from the boat, framed by sparkling turquoise water and lush greenery, it's hard not to feel a spark of excitement.

Getting to Marathonisi is part of the fun. Boats leave regularly from the nearby villages of Keri and Laganas, offering both group tours and private rentals. The ride across the bay is short and scenic, and you might even spot one of the famous Caretta caretta turtles gliding beneath the surface. Some tours pause to let you snorkel in the clear shallows before reaching the island. Once you arrive, the beach invites you in with its calm, crystal-clear water and peaceful atmosphere. The shoreline is perfect for swimming, sunbathing, or just floating on your back while gazing at the sky.

Behind the beach, steep green cliffs rise dramatically, and small sea caves wait around the edges for a bit of exploring by kayak or paddleboard.

Because Marathonisi is a protected part of the National Marine Park, there are no beach bars or buildings, just pure, natural beauty. Visitors are asked to respect the environment, especially during the turtle nesting season when parts of the sand are roped off to protect buried eggs. That quiet, respectful vibe only adds to the charm of the place. It feels special like a secret corner of the island reserved just for those who make the journey.

Spending a few hours on Turtle Island is a refreshing break from the busier beach scenes. The water sparkles, the atmosphere is peaceful, and the connection to nature is real. If you're craving a day that's both relaxing and unforgettable, Marathonisi delivers that rare mix of calm and awe.

Mizithres Rocks and Sea Views

Mizithres Rocks is one of those places that stops you in your tracks. Towering limestone formations rise out of the sea like nature's own sculptures, set against a backdrop of dazzling blue water that shifts color with the sun. These striking twin rocks, located at the far southern tip of Zakynthos, near Keri, are pure drama raw, beautiful, and wildly photogenic.

The best way to take in this jaw-dropping sight is from the panoramic viewpoint above, near the Keri Lighthouse. It's an easy drive from Zakynthos Town just follow the road signs to Keri and then continue toward the lighthouse. Once you arrive, get ready for one of the most breathtaking sea views on the island. From this cliffside perch, you'll see the Mizithres Rocks jutting up from the glowing blue below, looking almost surreal against the open Ionian Sea. The light at sunset turns everything gold, and the water takes on an almost magical glow. This is one photo you'll want to frame.

For those craving a closer look, boat trips departing from Keri Beach offer the chance to sail right up to the rocks and even swim near the secluded pebble beaches that have formed between them. The water here is unbelievably clear and deep turquoise, making it a dream spot for snorkeling. The contrast between the sheer white cliffs and the glowing blue water is something you won't forget.

Mizithres is still somewhat under the radar, so the crowds are fewer, and the experience feels refreshingly wild. It's the kind of place that instantly connects you to the island's raw, natural beauty. If you're chasing unforgettable views and a feeling of awe, standing above or sailing below the Mizithres Rocks is absolutely unmissable.

Askos Stone Park

Askos Stone Park is a delightful escape into the natural heart of Zakynthos. Nestled near the village of Volimes in the island's lush northern region, this peaceful spot is a charming blend of wildlife sanctuary, botanical haven, and traditional stone architecture. It's the kind of place that makes you slow down, breathe deeply, and really take in the world around you.

Once you arrive about a 45-minute drive from Zakynthos Town the first thing you'll notice is the sense of quiet. Surrounded by pine trees, olive groves, and old stone walls, the park feels like a step back in time. As you stroll along its shady paths, you'll come across deer grazing, peacocks strutting proudly, and turtles lounging near freshwater springs. Goats, rabbits, and even ponies make friendly appearances, and it's all set against a backdrop of traditional Zakynthian stone structures built without cement, just as they were centuries ago.

The park is not a zoo, it's a thoughtfully designed space where animals roam freely, and native plants are carefully preserved. There's a deep respect here for the environment, which makes it especially rewarding for travelers looking for more than just a pretty view. Kids love the hands-on feel of the park, and adults appreciate the quiet beauty and the gentle pace. Keep your eyes open for the old stone wells and wine presses tucked among the trees; they add a fascinating cultural layer to the experience.

Askos Stone Park is open year-round, and it's easy to reach by car or as part of a guided tour from many parts of the island. The staff are warm and welcoming, often sharing stories about the animals or the history of the park itself. It's one of Zakynthos' lesser-known treasures, a place where nature and tradition meet in the most charming way. If you're craving a peaceful break from the beach or a chance to connect with the island's authentic soul, this park is a breath of fresh air.

Korakonissi Cove

Korakonissi Cove is one of Zakynthos' most dramatic natural wonders untamed, rugged, and absolutely breathtaking. Tucked away near the village of Agios Leon on the island's wild western coast, this hidden spot doesn't draw crowds like the big-name beaches, which is exactly why it feels so special. The drive here is an adventure in itself, winding through olive groves and quiet hills until you reach a rocky path that drops down to the sea.

Once you arrive, you'll see it: a spectacular natural stone arch towering over crystal-clear turquoise water, carved out by time and the force of the Ionian Sea. This isn't a sandy beach with umbrellas, Korakonissi is a raw, rocky cove made for the bold and curious. The water is unbelievably clear and deep, making it a favorite for cliff diving and snorkeling. Sunlight dances off the surface, casting flickers of light onto the rocks below, while the crashing waves echo against the walls of the natural arch.

There's something ancient and untamed about this place. You can sit on the rocks and just watch the sea, or scramble down closer to the water for a swim that feels like a secret. The adventurous will want to explore the underwater caves and crevices, which hide sea urchins, fish, and vibrant marine life. Strong swimmers will have a blast here, but it's not ideal for small children or those needing calm water, so keep that in mind.

Getting to Korakonissi takes about 45 minutes from Zakynthos Town by car, and you'll want sturdy shoes for the rocky terrain. There's a small parking area at the top, but from there, it's all walking. Bring water, sunscreen, and a sense of curiosity—this is a place for explorers. There's also a rustic taverna nearby where you can reward yourself with grilled octopus or a cold drink after your dip.

Olive Groves & Zakynthian Countryside

The olive groves of Zakynthos stretch across the island like a living tapestry, telling stories of tradition, endurance, and beauty with every twist of a gnarled branch. Driving through the countryside, especially around villages like Lithakia, Kiliomenos, or Katastari, you'll find yourself surrounded by endless rows of ancient trees. Their silver-green leaves shimmer under the sun, and the soft rustling of the branches in the breeze creates a kind of quiet music that perfectly matches the slow rhythm of rural island life.

This part of Zakynthos feels worlds away from the beaches and resorts. Here, the land is dotted with stone cottages, hand-built walls, sleepy donkeys in the shade, and family-run farms that seem untouched by time. You'll spot locals tending to their groves with a kind of calm focus passed down through generations, and in harvest season, nets cover the ground as olives are gently gathered for pressing. Many of these trees are centuries old, their twisted trunks like sculptures shaped by the winds of history.

Exploring the Zakynthian countryside on foot or by car gives you a chance to connect deeply with the island. Quiet roads wind through rolling hills and fields of wildflowers in spring, while olive oil shops and tasting rooms welcome visitors year-round. Stop into one of the small presses to try freshly made olive oil, peppery, golden, and smooth and you'll understand why it's considered some of the best in Greece. The locals are proud of their product and often happy to share the secrets behind its flavor.

You can reach the island's countryside by driving inland from any coastal base; most villages are only 20 to 40 minutes from Zakynthos Town or the main beach resorts. Rent a car, hop on a bike, or take a guided tour through the olive estates and vineyards. The scenery is ever-changing and unspoiled, with moments that feel pulled from a postcard. Along the way, you might stumble upon a small chapel tucked beneath the trees, or a roadside stall selling honey and herbs from the hills.

Best Things to Do in Zakynthos

Zakynthos is one of those places that effortlessly blends jaw-dropping natural beauty, authentic village life, and unforgettable experiences. No matter what kind of traveler you are, sun-chaser, foodie, adventurer, or history lover there's something here that will win you over completely. The island is packed with gems, from dramatic cliffs to tranquil coves, and the best way to discover it is by mixing a little exploration with some good old-fashioned relaxation.

Zakynthos isn't just a destination, it's an experience. And the best way to enjoy it is to follow the rhythm of the island, take your time, and let each day surprise you.

ADVENTURE & OUTDOOR ACTIVITIES

Zakynthos is more than just beautiful beaches and postcard-perfect views; it's a full-blown playground for anyone craving a little adventure. The island's wild cliffs, turquoise waters, and rolling countryside make it a dream destination if you're itching to get active and experience nature in the most thrilling ways.

If you're a fan of the sea, you're in luck. Snorkeling and scuba diving around Zakynthos offer a close-up look at a vivid underwater world.

The waters are so clear that even with just a mask and fins, you'll spot colorful fish darting through sea caves and maybe even a sea turtle gliding by. There are dive centers in places like Laganas, Keri, and Agios Sostis where you can book guided dives or take a beginner's course. The marine life here is protected, so every trip under the surface feels like a respectful journey into a hidden ecosystem.

Snorkeling & Scuba Diving

The waters around Zakynthos are more than just striking shades of blue; they're an entire world waiting to be explored. For snorkeling and scuba diving fans, the island offers some of the most breathtaking underwater spots in Greece. Two standout locations are the Blue Caves in the north and the Keri Caves in the south. Both promise dazzling seascapes, surreal rock formations, and encounters with vibrant marine life.

To reach the Blue Caves, head to the northern tip of the island near Skinari. From here, small boats and diving excursions depart regularly, especially from Agios Nikolaos port. Even before you hit the water, the sight of these caves is something special white limestone arches framing an impossibly blue sea. The way sunlight bounces off the cave walls and reflects in the water creates a glow that doesn't feel real. Snorkeling here is like floating through liquid sapphire. If you're scuba diving, you can explore deeper crevices and tunnels, where fish dart through the shadows and shafts of light pour down like spotlights from above.

On the opposite end of the island, near the charming village of Keri, the Keri Caves are another unmissable underwater treasure. The best way to get here is by boat from Limni Keri harbor. These caves are wilder and more dramatic, with towering cliffs and arches that plunge straight into the sea. Snorkeling here gives you up-close views of dramatic underwater rock shapes, shimmering schools of fish, and maybe even a passing turtle. For scuba divers, the caves offer exciting swim-throughs and ledges where octopuses and colorful sponges hide.

Both sites are suitable for all levels. You'll find diving schools and guided tours that cater to beginners as well as seasoned divers. Many offer combo trips that include snorkeling, swimming, and even a chance to stop at hidden coves along the way. Every second spent beneath the surface in Zakynthos feels like stepping into a secret world. The colors, the silence, the movement, it's all hypnotic.

Sea Kayaking

Sea kayaking in Zakynthos is a breathtaking way to experience the island from a whole new perspective. The moment your paddle dips into the crystal-clear water and your kayak glides past dramatic cliffs and hidden coves, it's easy to see why this adventure is a favorite among nature lovers. It's quiet, peaceful, and gives you front-row access to some of the island's most enchanting coastal spots that are unreachable by road.

One of the most exciting routes begins from Limni Keri in the south. From here, you can kayak along the limestone coastline toward the magnificent Keri Caves. These towering sea caves are a true spectacle, with arches, tunnels, and openings where sunlight filters through, lighting up the turquoise water beneath you. The cliffs are wild and rugged, and you might spot seabirds nesting high above or even a curious loggerhead turtle swimming nearby. It's the kind of paddle that keeps your eyes wide and your camera ready.

Another beautiful stretch to explore by kayak is around the Vasilikos Peninsula. This area offers gentler waters and is perfect for beginners or anyone looking for a relaxing trip. You'll float past pine-covered hills, secluded beaches, and calm bays where you can stop for a swim or a picnic. The coastline is unspoiled and quiet, giving you that off-the-grid feeling without ever being too far from a small taverna or village.

If you want to join a guided trip, several local outfitters offer half-day and full-day tours, including equipment and support boats for safety. Some trips even start early in the morning or near sunset for a magical golden-light experience. Most tours depart from the southern coast, especially from areas like Agios Sostis, Limni Keri, and Porto Roma. It's a good idea to book ahead in peak summer months to secure your spot.

Sea kayaking is more than just paddling along the water. It's about discovering quiet corners of Zakynthos that many visitors miss, getting up close to nature, and feeling the rhythm of the sea. The combination of physical activity, stunning scenery, and complete freedom makes it one of the most rewarding ways to explore the island.

Hiking Trails (e.g., Skopos Mountain)

Hiking on Zakynthos is a thrilling way to connect with the island's raw, natural beauty, and one of the most rewarding trails takes you straight to the top of Skopos Mountain. Rising proudly above the Vasilikos Peninsula, this hike is a true gem for outdoor lovers craving a panoramic view and a touch of adventure. The path climbs steadily through a patchwork of wild herbs, olive groves, and fragrant pine trees, each turn offering a more stunning view than the last.

To start your hike up Skopos Mountain, head to the village of Argassi, which lies just a short drive south of Zakynthos Town. From there, a narrow dirt trail winds up the slope, with signs pointing you in the right direction. The ascent is moderate but steady, making it a perfect challenge for casual hikers who want to break a sweat while still enjoying the journey. As you climb, the island begins to unfold beneath your feet lush valleys, glittering coastline, and sleepy villages in the distance.

At the summit, you'll find the small and weathered Monastery of Panagia Skopiotissa. The structure itself is a charming relic, with faded frescoes and arched stone walls that seem to echo the peaceful silence around you. But the real reward is the 360-degree view, absolutely breathtaking. You can see all the way across to the Peloponnese on a clear day, with the Ionian Sea stretching endlessly into the horizon. The contrast of rugged mountains and deep blue water is unforgettable.

The descent offers a chance to spot wildflowers, butterflies, and even the occasional goat balancing confidently on the rocks. If you're hiking in spring or early summer, the trails are especially vibrant with color and buzzing with life. Be sure to bring water, sturdy shoes, and a hat for the sun, as much of the trail is exposed.

Jeep Safari Tours

If you're craving a bold, off-the-beaten-path way to discover Zakynthos, a Jeep safari tour is the perfect adventure. These guided excursions take you deep into the rugged interior of the island, where hidden villages, winding mountain tracks, and sweeping coastal views await.

It's not just a scenic drive, it's a hands-on journey through wild, untamed landscapes and authentic island culture. Most Jeep safaris start from Zakynthos Town or the southern resorts like Laganas or Kalamaki, with hotel pickup included for ease.

You'll hop into a 4x4 vehicle often shared with a small group and set off on dusty backroads that weave through olive groves, rocky hills, and forested trails. The feeling of bouncing along uneven terrain with the salty breeze whipping through the open windows is thrilling and unforgettable.

The routes vary slightly depending on the company, but a common highlight is the drive up to Mount Vrachionas, the island's highest point. From here, you get a breathtaking panoramic view that stretches across Zakynthos and out to the Ionian Sea. Some tours also wind through remote villages like Loucha and Gyri, where life moves slowly and traditions still hold strong. You'll get a chance to stop, snap photos, chat with locals, and perhaps taste fresh local honey or handmade cheese.

One of the most exciting parts of the safari is reaching viewpoints that regular rental cars can't access. You might pull up to a cliffside ledge with the wild sea crashing far below, or pause beneath towering cypress trees while your guide explains local myths and history. Some tours also include stops at historical monasteries, natural springs, or even a hidden beach for a refreshing dip.

Expect plenty of laughter, a few bumps along the way, and a full day of storytelling, exploration, and jaw-dropping views. Jeep safaris are ideal if you're looking for a different side of Zakynthos, one that's raw, untamed, and full of character. It's an unmissable way to see the island's soul beyond the beaches, with every twist and turn offering a new surprise.

Horseback Riding on the Beach

Riding a horse along the golden sands of Zakynthos as the sun begins to dip into the Ionian Sea is one of those pinch-me travel moments that stays with you long after the trip ends. Horseback riding on the beach offers a dreamy, almost cinematic way to connect with the island's natural beauty and it's easier to arrange than you might think.

Most rides begin in the southern part of Zakynthos, particularly around Kalamaki and Laganas. Several local stables offer well-cared-for horses and knowledgeable guides who pair you with the right mount based on your skill level. No previous experience? No problem. The rides are tailored for all levels, from first-timers to seasoned riders, with safety and comfort as top priorities. Once you're saddled up, you'll follow gentle trails that wind through olive groves or sand dunes before reaching the beach. And then comes the magic: the moment your horse steps onto the soft shoreline, with nothing but open coast ahead. The sound of hooves in the wet sand, the salty breeze brushing your face, and the sparkling water just beside you it's peaceful, exhilarating, and completely unforgettable all at once.

Sunset rides are especially popular, and for good reason. As the sky turns gold and the sea reflects those warm hues, the setting becomes something truly special. Some routes even pass through protected nesting areas for loggerhead turtles (Caretta caretta), which adds a powerful reminder of the island's rich natural life.

Tours can be arranged directly with local stables or through hotels and travel agents. They usually include transportation to the starting point and range from one to two hours. Riders are often treated to quiet moments off the beaten path, well away from the crowds.

This is not just a photo opportunity, it's a chance to slow down, breathe in the moment, and see Zakynthos from a unique perspective. Galloping through the surf or gently walking beside the waves, horseback riding on the beach is a heart-stirring experience that lets you feel the island's magic, one hoofbeat at a time.

Boat Tours Around the Island

There's no better way to grasp the full beauty of Zakynthos than from the water. A boat tour around the island opens up a whole world of stunning coastlines, sea caves, hidden beaches, and postcard-perfect views that you simply can't get from land. It's a day packed with discovery, fresh sea air, and unforgettable stops along the way.

Tours typically depart from Zakynthos Town, Agios Sostis, or Laganas port. You can join a group cruise or book a private boat for a more personalized adventure. Some boats are sleek and modern, others are charming and traditional, but all of them promise an experience that showcases Zakynthos at its dazzling best.

One of the highlights is the world-famous Navagio Beach, also known as Shipwreck Beach. As your boat approaches, the towering cliffs give way to a strip of pure white sand and the rusting skeleton of the shipwreck nestled at its center. It's an iconic sight, and being there in person surrounded by sheer rock faces and brilliant turquoise water feels utterly surreal.

Another breathtaking stop is the Blue Caves, a string of natural arches carved into the cliffs by the sea. As your boat glides through them, the sunlight bouncing off the water lights up the caves in glowing shades of blue. It's a photographer's dream and a feast for the eyes. Many tours also include a visit to Marathonisi Island, a lush, turtle-shaped islet off the southern coast. Depending on the season, you might even spot loggerhead sea turtles swimming nearby. Some itineraries include snorkeling breaks, beach stops, or even a swim inside one of the sea caves, so bring a swimsuit and towel.

Boat tours usually last between three and eight hours, depending on the route. You can find departures in the morning, midday, or for a golden-hour cruise around sunset. Booking is simple, most are offered through local travel agencies, hotels, or directly at the harbor.

Exploring Zakynthos by boat is more than just a fun outing; it's a vivid, ever-changing journey along one of Greece's most breathtaking coastlines. The water glistens, the cliffs rise dramatically, and every turn reveals another stunning scene.

Sunset Cruises

A sunset cruise around Zakynthos is pure magic. There's something unforgettable about watching the sky slowly transform into a canvas of deep golds, fiery reds, and soft pinks, all while gliding across calm Ionian waters. It's a peaceful, romantic, and wildly beautiful moment that lingers in your memory long after the sun has dipped below the horizon.

These cruises usually set sail from Zakynthos Town, Agios Sostis, or the marina in Laganas in the late afternoon. You'll board a comfortable boat, some sleek and modern, others more classic and intimate and head out to sea just as the heat of the day starts to fade. The breeze is gentle, the light is golden, and the vibe is easygoing and relaxed. The routes often pass by some of the island's most scenic coastal spots, such as the Keri Lighthouse cliffs or the sweeping bay near Marathonisi. Some boats pause at panoramic viewpoints to let you soak in the surroundings and take in the sheer beauty of Zakynthos bathed in sunset colors. On a clear evening, the horizon seems to melt into the sea, creating a view so breathtaking it feels like time stops.

Many cruises offer drinks on board, maybe a chilled glass of wine or a refreshing cocktail and sometimes light snacks or dinner are served. It's the perfect way to unwind after a day of exploring. Couples especially love this experience, but it's also a wonderful way for solo travelers and families to wind down and see the island from a fresh perspective.

Booking is easy through local tour companies, hotel desks, or even right at the port. Just be sure to bring a light jacket for the breezy return and, of course, your camera because no filter could ever match the real colors you'll see out there on the water.

A sunset cruise isn't just another item on a travel itinerary. It's one of those rare moments that feels both peaceful and electric. You'll feel the hush of the ocean, the warmth of the fading light, and the simple joy of watching nature put on one of its most dazzling displays. It's easily one of the most rewarding ways to end your day on Zakynthos.

Paragliding at Kalamaki

Paragliding at Kalamaki is one of the boldest and most thrilling ways to experience Zakynthos. As your feet lift off the golden sand and the wind carries you over the island's southern coast, you're hit with a wave of freedom that's hard to put into words. The sweeping views of the turquoise Ionian Sea, the long stretch of Kalamaki Beach, and the rolling hills beyond create a panorama that feels straight out of a dream.

The take-off point is usually right on Kalamaki Beach, where local operators set you up with experienced instructors and all the gear you need. After a short safety briefing, you're strapped in and ready to soar. The process is smooth and friendly, even for first-timers. And once you're airborne, the silence and stillness up there is just as thrilling as the height.

From above, you'll spot Caretta caretta turtle nesting sites along the coast, the gentle curve of Laganas Bay, and if you're lucky, a few turtles swimming beneath the surface. The contrast between the deep blue of the sea and the soft greens of the inland hills is stunning. You'll feel like you're floating between worlds, with the sun on your face and the sea breeze brushing past you.

Most flights last around 10 to 15 minutes, but those minutes pack a punch. Every second is filled with adrenaline and awe. And the landing, smooth and controlled, brings you gently back down to the warm sand where it all began.

Kalamaki is just a 10-minute drive from Zakynthos Town and easy to reach by car, taxi, or even by bike if you're up for it. The beach itself is laid-back and welcoming, so you can plan your flight around a relaxed beach day. There are sunbeds, cafes, and places to grab a drink or snack once you're back on solid ground.

TURTLE SPOTTING EXPERIENCES

Turtle spotting in Zakynthos is one of those unforgettable experiences that sticks with you long after your trip ends. The island is one of the most important nesting grounds for the endangered Caretta caretta sea turtle, and seeing these gentle giants in their natural habitat is both magical and moving.

Caretta Caretta Turtle Watching Tours

Caretta Caretta turtle watching tours in Zakynthos are the kind of experience that makes a holiday feel truly special. These tours focus on spotting the island's most famous residents, the loggerhead sea turtles right in their natural element, and there's no better place to do it than Laganas Bay and around Marathonisi, also known as Turtle Island.

Laganas Bay is part of the National Marine Park, a protected zone set up specifically to help safeguard the turtles' breeding grounds. You'll board a small boat with glass bottoms and set out across the calm, shallow waters where the turtles often swim just beneath the surface. It doesn't take long before someone spots one gliding gracefully near the boat or popping up for air. They're surprisingly large, with broad shells and slow, deliberate movements that make them look almost prehistoric.

Marathonisi is just across the bay and shaped like a turtle itself, which makes it an iconic stop during the tours. Boats often anchor nearby to give visitors time to swim or snorkel near the shoreline, though landing on the nesting beach is usually restricted during breeding season to protect the turtles and their fragile eggs. Even so, the views from the water are stunning soft golden sand, turquoise water, and rocky coves that feel far from the busy world.

Tours typically leave from Laganas harbor or Agios Sostis and last about two to three hours. Most run in the morning or late afternoon, when the turtles are most active and the light on the water is picture-perfect. Guides are knowledgeable and respectful, making sure the boats stay a safe distance while still offering excellent viewing opportunities. You'll learn about the turtles' nesting habits, their long journeys across the Mediterranean, and the threats they face from pollution and habitat loss.

The best part is that this is more than just a sightseeing trip. Watching a Caretta Caretta swim freely through the clear Ionian Sea is a reminder of how rare and precious these moments can be. It's a quiet thrill, peaceful, unforgettable, and something you'll be talking about long after you've left the island behind.

Eco-friendly Turtle Conservation Tours

Eco-friendly turtle conservation tours in Zakynthos offer something deeper than just sightseeing; they give you a front-row seat to meaningful environmental work, all while showing you the beauty of the island's natural world. These tours aren't just about spotting sea turtles from a boat. They're about understanding the delicate balance that keeps these creatures safe and learning how tourism can be a powerful force for protection rather than harm.

Led by conservationists and trained guides, these tours often start with a short briefing. You'll hear about the efforts being made to protect the endangered loggerhead turtles, locally known as Caretta Caretta, and get a close look at the nesting beaches where they lay their eggs. Conservation-focused tours don't crowd the beaches or disturb the turtles. Instead, they follow strict rules that keep human interaction to a minimum. You might walk carefully along Laganas Beach at sunrise with a guide pointing out turtle tracks, or observe nesting zones from a respectful distance using binoculars.

Some tours are hosted in collaboration with local organizations like ARCHELON, the Sea Turtle Protection Society of Greece. These programs often include access to research stations or eco-centers where you can see the day-to-day efforts of volunteers recording hatchling numbers, monitoring nests, and even rescuing injured turtles. For anyone curious about marine biology or conservation, this behind-the-scenes access is fascinating and eye-opening.

You'll likely explore the Marine Park of Zakynthos, especially the southern coast around Kalamaki, Marathonisi, and Gerakas, where the highest number of nests are found. All transportation is done with eco-conscious practices in mind, using quieter, smaller boats to avoid disturbing marine life. The guides are usually locals who know the island well and are passionate about preserving its wildlife. Their stories and insights add depth to every moment.

FAMILY-FRIENDLY ACTIVITIES

Zakynthos is packed with fun, relaxed, and memory-making moments for families of all kinds. The island offers the perfect blend of outdoor adventure, safe swimming spots, gentle animal encounters, and cultural experiences that even kids can appreciate. Days here can be both exciting and easygoing, ideal for letting kids burn off energy while adults unwind in stunning surroundings.

Water Village (Amusement Water Park)

Water Village in Sarakinado is hands-down one of the most exciting places to spend a sun-soaked day in Zakynthos, especially if you're traveling with kids or just a kid at heart. It's the island's largest water park, and from the moment you step through the gates, the sound of rushing water, excited laughter, and upbeat music sets the tone for a day packed with fun.

The park is a vibrant sprawl of colorful slides, lazy rivers, splash pools, and sun loungers. There's something for every level of thrill-seeker. Daredevils can shoot down high-speed rides like the Free Fall or the Mat Racer, where your stomach flips and you can't help but scream and laugh all the way down. For those who like to take it slower, the Lazy River winds gently through leafy corners of the park, letting you float with the current under the Zakynthian sun.

Families with younger kids won't be left out. The children's play zones are brilliant, full of mini slides, shallow pools, climbing nets, and gigantic tipping buckets that send waves of water crashing down to endless giggles. Everything is built with safety in mind, with lifeguards keeping a close watch and plenty of shaded areas to cool off when the midday heat kicks in.

It's easy to spend the whole day here. There are plenty of food and drink options inside the park, from quick snacks to full meals. Prices are reasonable, and there's no need to leave the park to refuel. Lockers, changing rooms, and sunbeds are available for rent, so you can store your things and relax without dragging a bag around all day.

Getting to Water Village is simple. It's located in Sarakinado, just a 10- to 15-minute drive from Zakynthos Town, and many resorts and hotels offer shuttle services or easy taxi access. If you're driving, there's ample parking right outside the gates.

Water Village isn't just a break from sightseeing, it's a full-on day of splashing, sliding, and laughing until your cheeks hurt. It's a refreshing way to beat the heat and one of those places where everyone from toddlers to grandparents finds a reason to smile.

Fantasy Mini Golf

Fantasy Mini Golf in Tsilivi is one of those places that turns a simple game into an all-out adventure. It's colorful, playful, and packed with fun, making it a fantastic stop for families, groups of friends, or couples looking to mix a little competition with plenty of laughs.

What makes this mini golf spot stand out is the sheer creativity of the courses. You're not just putting a ball through a few obstacles, you're navigating pirate ships, ancient ruins, tropical gardens, and even a spooky graveyard. Each of the themed zones has been designed with incredible attention to detail, from cascading waterfalls to quirky statues, which gives the whole place a charming, almost storybook feel.

The venue offers four different 18-hole courses, and you can choose one or go for a combo deal and play through them all. Some holes are tricky and test your aim, while others are just plain silly in the best way. There's a relaxed, friendly vibe throughout the place, so even if you've never played before, you'll feel right at home picking up a club and jumping in.

It's open until late in the evening, so it's a great post-dinner activity when the sun has cooled off and you're looking for something fun to do. At night, the place lights up beautifully with colorful LEDs, making the entire course look even more magical.

Olive Oil Factory Tours

Visiting an olive oil factory in Zakynthos is like stepping into the heart of the island's traditions. These tours are not only fascinating, they're also delicious, giving you a deeper appreciation for the golden liquid that flows through Greek cuisine.

Most of the olive oil factories are tucked into the countryside, surrounded by age-old olive trees that have been producing fruit for generations. One of the most popular spots is Aristeon Olive Press, located in Lithakia. It's easy to reach by car or scooter, and many local tour companies also offer guided visits that include transport. As soon as you step inside, the cool scent of fresh olives welcomes you. You'll be guided through the production process, where you'll see everything from the centuries-old grinding stones to the sleek modern machines that press the olives today. It's a great mix of history and innovation, showing how Zakynthians have preserved their heritage while embracing new techniques.

The highlight, of course, is the tasting. Freshly pressed extra virgin olive oil is poured into tiny cups so you can sip and savor its smooth, peppery notes. Some factories even offer oil infused with garlic, lemon, or herbs, and they're often paired with fresh bread, olives, or local cheese to complete the experience. There's a small shop on-site where you can buy bottles straight from the source, often at better prices than you'll find in town.

These make perfect souvenirs or gifts, and you'll know you're taking home something truly authentic. Factory tours usually take less than an hour, so they're easy to fit into a day of sightseeing or exploring nearby villages. It's a slow-paced, sensory-rich experience ideal for travelers who enjoy getting a taste of local life in a relaxed, meaningful way.

Glass-Bottom Boat Tours

Glass-bottom boat tours in Zakynthos are a laid-back and scenic way to explore the island's stunning underwater world without even getting your feet wet. These boats glide across the crystal-clear Ionian Sea, giving you a front-row seat to a vibrant marine show right beneath your feet.

Most tours depart from Laganas, Agios Sostis, or Porto Vromi, and they're easy to join by booking at the waterfront or through a local travel agency. The boats are designed with wide, transparent panels in the floor, so as soon as you set off, you can gaze down at schools of fish darting through the seagrass, colorful reefs, and the occasional loggerhead turtle cruising through the blue.

One of the most popular routes includes stops at Marathonisi, better known as Turtle Island, and the stunning Keri Caves. As you drift past dramatic cliffs and luminous turquoise waters, the captain usually slows down so you can peer deep into sea caves and rocky crevices.

Some tours also offer a quick swim stop, giving you a chance to splash into the water while anchored near secluded coves. The ride itself is smooth and relaxing, with the breeze and sun adding to the charm. It's a great option for families with young kids or anyone who prefers to stay dry while still getting a close-up view of the island's natural beauty.

Most tours last around two to three hours, which leaves plenty of time to explore other parts of the island afterward. Just don't forget your camera. The views from the boat, both above and below the surface, are unforgettable.

CULTURAL & CULINARY EXPERIENCES

Zakynthos isn't just about sea caves and sunsets, it's also packed with flavor, tradition, and heart. The island's culture is rich with centuries-old customs, music that stirs the soul, and food that will have you asking for seconds.

Start by exploring the local villages tucked into the hills and countryside. Places like Volimes and Kiliomenos still move to a slower rhythm, where you can watch artisans weaving baskets or painting religious icons by hand. It's in these villages that local hospitality really shines. You might be invited in for a coffee or offered a taste of homemade wine without even asking.

When it comes to food, Zakynthos is all about honest, bold flavors. Think grilled meats sizzling over open flames, creamy local cheeses, garden-fresh vegetables tossed in wild oregano, and golden olive oil made just steps away from the table. Traditional taverns, many family-run for generations, serve up hearty dishes like rabbit stew, Zakynthian ladotyri cheese, and savory pies filled with greens and herbs. Dining here is rarely rushed. It's about connection, conversation, and that wonderful moment when the wine flows and someone pulls out a guitar.

For a deeper experience, look for cooking classes held in rural homes or olive farms. These hands-on sessions let you roll dough for village-style pies or stuff tomatoes with herbs straight from the garden. It's a fun, delicious way to learn about Greek culinary traditions.

You can also visit one of the island's many wineries or olive oil estates. Most offer tastings that let you try their products paired with local snacks. Touring a small olive press or walking through rows of centuries-old trees gives you a fresh appreciation for the flavors that define Zakynthian life.

Live music and festivals are another highlight. Traditional kantades romantic serenades sung in harmony still echo through the island streets during summer evenings. If you're lucky enough to be around during a village celebration, expect dancing, food that keeps coming, and a joy that's downright contagious.

Zakynthian Wine Tasting Tours

Zakynthos may be known for its turquoise seas and sandy beaches, but its wine scene is a hidden treasure that deserves your full attention. The island's sun-soaked hills and mineral-rich soil produce grapes that pack incredible character, and local winemakers are turning that into bottles full of bold flavor and personality.

Joining a wine tasting tour in Zakynthos isn't just about sipping, it's a journey into the island's soul. You'll find small, family-run vineyards where traditions stretch back generations, and each wine tells a story. Most tours take you beyond the tasting room. You'll walk through rows of vines under a wide open sky, step into rustic cellars filled with the scent of aging oak barrels, and hear passionate winemakers talk about how each vintage comes to life.

One standout is the Vertzami grape, native to Zakynthos and used to make rich, dark red wines with depth and a touch of spice. There's also Avgoustiatis, another local favorite, which produces smooth, elegant reds. Many vineyards also craft whites that are crisp and fresh perfect for warm Mediterranean days.

Most wine tours start from Zakynthos Town or popular villages like Lithakia or Kampi. Some can be booked through local tour companies, while others are hosted directly by the estates themselves. Transfers are often included, so you can relax and enjoy each glass without a second thought.

Tasting sessions typically include a lineup of wines paired with local delicacies cheese, olives, fresh bread, even sweet fig jams. It's a feast for the senses, not just your taste buds.

If you're lucky, you might visit during harvest season, when the vines are full and the energy in the air is something special. And if you've never toasted under the golden light of a Zakynthian sunset, surrounded by vineyards and new friends, it's time to change that. Wine tasting in Zakynthos isn't rushed. It invites you to slow down, savor every note, and discover a side of the island that lingers long after the last sip.

Olive Oil and Honey Tasting

Tasting olive oil and honey in Zakynthos is more than just a snack; it's a sensory experience wrapped in tradition, sunshine, and pure Greek flavor. This island has been producing both for centuries, and once you try them straight from the source, you'll never look at a supermarket bottle the same way again.

The olive oil here is liquid gold. Zakynthian olives are harvested with care and pressed quickly to lock in their rich, peppery flavor. Visiting a local olive mill lets you watch the whole process from the moment the olives are collected to the instant the fresh oil drips into gleaming tins. You'll sample different varieties, some smooth and buttery, others bold and grassy and learn how the taste can change depending on the olive type and harvest time.

Honey tastings are equally enchanting. Local beekeepers will walk you through the fragrant world of wild thyme, pine, and heather honey, each offering a different taste of Zakynthos' untouched countryside. The bees here feed on herbs and flowers native to the island, which gives the honey a complexity and depth that store-bought jars just can't touch.

Many small farms and family-run estates welcome visitors for guided tastings, usually set against stunning backdrops of olive groves or mountain slopes. You'll be served fresh bread, cheeses, and seasonal fruit alongside your tastings, making it feel more like a countryside picnic than a tour. Some spots even offer hands-on experiences like picking olives or watching bees at work in transparent hives.

You can reach these farms by car from Zakynthos Town or any of the main resort villages. A few tour operators offer half-day culinary experiences that include both olive oil and honey stops, often paired with local wines and homemade snacks.

This kind of tasting isn't just delicious, it's grounded, personal, and deeply connected to the rhythms of the land. You walk away not just with new flavors on your tongue, but stories in your pocket and maybe even a bottle or two to savor back home.

Traditional Cooking Classes

Joining a traditional cooking class in Zakynthos is a delightful way to connect with the island's culture and eat very, very well. Instead of just dining out, you step into a local kitchen, tie on an apron, and get your hands into real Greek recipes passed down through generations.

These classes are often led by home cooks or chefs who've grown up making these dishes with their families. You won't just be following a recipe, you'll hear the stories behind the food, learn which herbs grow in the backyard, and discover how Zakynthians make use of every ingredient in the most flavorful way possible. Picture kneading dough for homemade pita, stuffing vine leaves with rice and herbs, or slow-cooking lamb in the traditional clay pot. One popular dish that tends to show up is "pastitsada," a rich, spiced meat stew, and if you're lucky, you might try your hand at making cheese pies or semolina desserts flavored with orange and honey.

Many of these classes take place in scenic village homes, garden terraces, or rustic farm kitchens surrounded by olive trees. Before the cooking begins, some hosts take you to the market or their own garden to pick fresh ingredients. It's the kind of experience that makes you feel like a guest rather than a tourist. Most classes are available in English and can be booked online or through your hotel.

Areas like Lagopodo, Maherado, and the villages around Alykes and Tsilivi offer wonderful options. You can drive yourself or arrange a transfer if you're staying farther out.

At the end of the class, you sit down to enjoy the meal you helped prepare, usually with a glass of local wine and the kind of laughter that only comes from cooking with others. It's warm, welcoming, and absolutely delicious and you'll leave with recipes and memories that last far longer than any souvenir.

Folk Music & Dance Nights

Folk music and dance nights in Zakynthos are pure magic. They're loud, lively, and overflowing with charm like being welcomed into a joyful family celebration where everyone's clapping, singing, and stamping their feet to the beat.

Held in village tavernas, open-air courtyards, and during local festivals, these evenings bring traditional Zakynthian culture to life in the most unforgettable way. The music is led by local musicians playing guitars, violins, and the bouzouki, that beloved Greek string instrument that seems to sing with emotion. You'll hear heartfelt island ballads alongside upbeat dance tunes that make it impossible to sit still for long. The dancing is just as captivating. Dancers in regional costumes flowing skirts, embroidered shirts, and sashes take the floor with proud, rhythmic steps.

You might catch a slow, graceful routine or a faster circle dance that pulls in the crowd. And don't be surprised if you're invited to join in. Even if your feet have no idea what they're doing, it's all about the fun. One of the best spots to experience this is in the villages of Volimes, Kiliomenos, or Gyri, where local tavernas host weekly cultural nights. Some organized tours also include dinner shows with folk performances, usually a generous feast of grilled meats, meze, and local wine, so your plate stays full while the music plays on.

Transportation is easy by rental car or taxi, especially since most of these events begin in the evening. If you're staying in popular areas like Tsilivi or Laganas, hotels often have partnerships with traditional venues and can arrange everything for you.

By the end of the night, you're clapping along, trying out a few dance steps, and completely caught up in the rhythm of island life. It's the kind of experience that brings people together with or without knowing the language and leaves you smiling all the way back to your hotel.

Local Markets & Artisan Shopping

Local markets and artisan shops in Zakynthos are a treasure trove of charm, color, and craftsmanship. They're the places where tradition is still very much alive and where you'll find keepsakes with real character, not just the usual tourist souvenirs.

Strolling through these markets is a treat for the senses. Stalls are brimming with handmade ceramics, colorful textiles, fragrant soaps made with local olive oil, and rows of golden honey that glow in the sun. You'll see old women selling bundles of oregano they dried themselves, and artisans carefully carving wood or painting delicate religious icons with astonishing detail. One of the best spots to explore is the main market in Zakynthos Town, near Solomos Square. It runs most mornings, especially busy on Saturdays. Here, you can pick up farm-fresh produce, local cheeses like ladotyri, and bottles of Zakynthian wine straight from the vineyard. It's the perfect place to chat with locals, practice a few Greek phrases, and get a real feel for the island's daily rhythm.

For something more tucked away and traditional, head up into the mountain villages Volimes is a standout. It's famous for its handwoven linens and embroidered tablecloths. You'll find cozy little shops operated by families who've passed their skills down through generations. They often make everything by hand, from goat milk soaps to leather sandals.

Getting to these places is easiest with a rental car, which gives you the freedom to explore small villages at your own pace. If you're staying in Zakynthos Town or Tsilivi, local buses and guided tours can also take you to some of the more artisan-focused spots. Shopping here isn't just about buying, it's about discovering the soul of the island through its crafts, its flavors, and the people who make them.

Zakynthos Town (Zante Town)

Zakynthos Town, often called Zante Town, is the vibrant heart of the island, a place where Venetian charm meets Greek soul in the most captivating way. This coastal capital hums with life, lined with pastel buildings, lively squares, and a harbor that glitters with bobbing boats and sea breezes.

Wander along the waterfront promenade and you'll feel the town's energy all around you. Cafés spill out onto the sidewalks, where locals sip coffee and watch the world go by. The air smells like fresh pastries from old bakeries, mingling with the scent of salt from the Ionian Sea. It's not just a place to pass through, it's a place to stay awhile, soak in the scenery, and let the pace of island life pull you in.

One of the town's highlights is Solomos Square, a wide, open plaza surrounded by neoclassical buildings and dotted with palm trees. It's home to the Byzantine Museum and a statue of Dionysios Solomos, the national poet of Greece. Just a few steps away, you'll find Saint Dionysios Church, the largest on the island, known for its richly painted ceilings and the silver casket of the island's patron saint. Shopping here is easy and pleasant, with pedestrian-friendly streets like Alexander Roma Street offering everything from high-end boutiques to shops filled with handmade goods, olive oil products, and local wine.

Stop by a tavern for a plate of Zakynthian rabbit stew or a creamy slice of mantolato nougat local flavors that will stay with you long after your trip. Getting to Zakynthos Town is straightforward. It's just a 10-minute drive from the airport, and buses connect it to all the major resorts across the island. If you're coming by ferry, the town's port is your first welcome to Zakynthos and it's a warm one.

This is a town that invites you to linger. It's the perfect blend of culture, coast, and character ideal for exploring, eating, shopping, or simply watching the sky turn golden over the harbor at sunset.

Strolling the Seafront Promenade

Strolling the seafront promenade in Zakynthos Town is one of those simple pleasures that feels utterly unforgettable. The moment your feet touch the smooth path that hugs the harbor, you're pulled into a rhythmic mix of sea air, sunlight, and the quiet buzz of daily island life.

The view alone is reason enough to walk it. On one side, boats gently bob on the sparkling Ionian Sea, their masts swaying in sync with the breeze. On the other, pastel-colored buildings, cozy cafés, and shaded benches invite you to slow down and soak it all in. During the golden hour, the promenade glows, the light dancing on the water and casting long, soft shadows across the pavement.

Locals and visitors mingle here, friends chatting over coffee, fishermen hauling in their nets, and couples walking hand-in-hand. It's the kind of place that doesn't demand anything from you. You can take your time, stop for a fresh scoop of gelato, or simply sit and gaze across the bay toward the mountains of the mainland. Getting here is effortless if you're staying in Zakynthos Town just head toward the port and follow the curve of the coastline. If you're arriving by ferry, the promenade is the very first thing to greet you. For those coming from nearby villages, buses and taxis drop off right near the harbor, making it an easy addition to your day.

It's not flashy or loud, but there's a certain magic in its calm. The promenade captures everything that makes Zakynthos special: natural beauty, laid-back atmosphere, and a sense of place you won't want to leave behind.

Shopping in Roma Street

Shopping on Roma Street in Zakynthos Town is like stepping into the island's heartbeat. This charming little street winds its way through the town center, lined with colorful storefronts, cheerful locals, and the irresistible scent of fresh pastries drifting out of bakeries. It's lively but not chaotic, buzzing with an energy that makes browsing feel more like a delightful adventure than an errand.

You'll find everything here from handcrafted leather sandals and delicate silver jewelry to vibrant ceramics and traditional Zakynthian products. Olive oil soaps, local honey, and spiced liqueurs crowd the shelves of tiny shops, each bottle and bar wrapped with care. Many of the stores are family-run, so don't be surprised if you're welcomed like an old friend and offered a sample of homemade treats or a story behind the product.

What makes Roma Street so enjoyable is the way it blends the old with the new. One moment you're passing a boutique selling chic beachwear, and the next you're standing in front of a store that's been selling handwoven linens for generations. The architecture around you keeps the atmosphere warm and inviting, with stone buildings, wooden shutters, and potted flowers brightening your path.

To get to Roma Street, just head into the heart of Zakynthos Town. It runs parallel to the seafront promenade and is only a short walk from Solomos Square. If you're staying in town, it's easy to find by foot. For those coming from other parts of the island, local buses and taxis drop off near the town center, and from there it's a quick stroll to this bustling strip.

This is the kind of shopping that stays with you. Not just for the bags you carry home, but for the little conversations, the textures, the laughter from a shopkeeper, and the sense that you're not just buying things you're part of something authentic and full of character.

Solomos & Kalvos Museum

Tucked just behind the buzz of Solomos Square, the Solomos & Kalvos Museum quietly preserves the literary soul of Zakynthos. This museum honors two of Greece's most important poets Dionysios Solomos, who wrote the Greek national anthem, and Andreas Kalvos, known for his passionate, classical verses. Visiting this museum isn't just a dip into history, it's a deep breath of the island's cultural pride.

The building itself has a warm, dignified presence. Inside, the rooms are lined with personal belongings, original manuscripts, rare books, and portraits that paint a vivid picture of the lives and times of these two literary giants. Solomos' writing desk and handwritten notes give you a raw, intimate connection to the creative process behind one of Greece's most cherished national symbols. The museum also hosts a rich archive of 18th and 19th-century Zakynthian life, complete with antique furniture, photographs, and even musical instruments from the period.

It's a quiet, thoughtful experience, one that invites you to slow down and take in the details. The exhibits are well-presented, and the staff is often eager to share stories that bring the poets to life in a way that's hard to find in textbooks. There's something incredibly moving about standing so close to the very pages where iconic verses were once scribbled down by hand.

Getting to the museum is easy. It's located right in Zakynthos Town, just steps from Solomos Square and a short walk from the seafront promenade. If you're staying nearby, it's the perfect place to wander into on a slow morning or afternoon. For those coming from elsewhere on the island, buses and taxis frequently service the town center.

A visit here adds a meaningful layer to your trip. It's not just about the sun and sea, but about the voices and stories that shaped modern Greece. This museum doesn't shout; it speaks softly and stays with you long after you leave.

Church of Agios Dionysios

The Church of Agios Dionysios is one of Zakynthos' most treasured landmarks, a striking blend of spiritual grandeur and island history that you can't miss as you stroll along the seafront in Zakynthos Town. With its impressive bell tower reaching toward the sky and its commanding position near the harbor, it stands as both a symbol of faith and a beacon of local pride.

Step through the doors and you're immediately surrounded by rich golden tones, dazzling chandeliers, and detailed frescoes that glow softly in the filtered light. The atmosphere is peaceful, even reverent, but never intimidating. This is the resting place of the island's patron saint, Agios Dionysios, and his silver casket is displayed in a beautifully adorned side chapel.

His story known for kindness and forgiveness still echoes strongly here, drawing not only devout pilgrims but curious travelers who want to connect with something deeper than the beach. The church survived the devastating 1953 earthquake, thanks to the protective efforts of locals who shielded it from destruction. It's been lovingly maintained since, and walking through it feels like moving through a living piece of Zakynthian resilience.

Getting here is simple. The church sits along the edge of Zakynthos Town, just a short walk from the main port and easily accessible by car, taxi, or even on foot if you're already exploring the town. It's usually open daily, and entry is free, though modest attire is recommended out of respect.

A visit to Agios Dionysios isn't just another sightseeing stop, it adds a deeper, more soulful dimension to your journey. It's the kind of place where time slows down, where history feels alive, and where the island's spirit quietly reveals itself.

Nightlife & Cafés

Zakynthos knows how to keep the energy alive after the sun goes down. The island's nightlife scene has a rhythm of its own, offering something for everyone from wild beach parties to cozy cafés perfect for winding down. It's one of those places where your night can begin with a relaxed espresso and end dancing under the stars.

Laganas is the heart of the party crowd. Clubs blast international hits, cocktails flow freely, and the atmosphere buzzes with excitement all night long. It's bold, electric, and unapologetically lively. If you're looking to let loose with a crowd, this is the spot. You'll find everything from open-air bars to booming nightclubs with DJs that keep the party going until sunrise.

For a more laid-back evening, Zakynthos Town delivers with charm. Rooftop lounges overlook the harbor, offering stunning sea views alongside chilled drinks and good conversation. Locals and visitors gather at stylish wine bars or hidden tavern corners where the music is low and the mood is relaxed. It's perfect for sipping a glass of local red or trying a traditional dessert while watching the town quietly sparkle.

Cafés across the island take full advantage of the balmy evenings. In places like Alykes, Argassi, or Tsilivi, you'll find beachside cafés where the sound of the waves keeps you company. Many stay open late, offering everything from creamy freddo cappuccinos to cocktails with fresh citrus and herbs. It's easy to spend hours chatting, people-watching, or simply soaking up the night air.

No matter your pace, Zakynthos has the perfect spot to enjoy the island after dark. From high-energy dancing to tranquil candlelit terraces, the island's nightlife and cafés promise unforgettable evenings that stretch long past sunset.

Hidden Gems in Zakynthos Town

Zakynthos Town may be the island's capital, but it still has secrets tucked away behind its lively squares and bustling harbor. Beyond the main streets, a quieter, more authentic side of town reveals itself in pockets that many travelers overlook. These hidden gems offer the kind of charm that sneaks up on you and lingers long after you leave.

Take a walk down narrow alleyways behind Solomos Square, and you'll stumble upon peaceful courtyards shaded by citrus trees. Locals gather here to chat on doorsteps, and you might find a tiny, family-run bakery selling still-warm koulouri or sweet mandolato candy. The scent of cinnamon and honey hangs in the air, pulling you toward shops that don't shout for attention but reward curiosity.

One such treasure is the tiny Church of St. Nicholas of the Mole. Sitting quietly by the harbor, it's easy to pass by, but step inside and you'll find aged frescoes and a peaceful vibe that feels a world away from the main promenade. It's a place for pausing, for letting time slow down.

Further up the hill, head toward Bochali for an unexpected treat. On the way to the viewpoint, you'll find old Venetian homes, quiet cafés with panoramic views, and almost no tourists around. Sit down for a coffee, and you'll feel like you've stepped into another era. This part of town feels more like a sleepy village than a capital.

Food & Drink in Zakynthos

Zakynthos is a place where food isn't just a meal, it's an experience wrapped in warm hospitality, bold Mediterranean flavors, and generations of tradition. Every bite on the island tells a story, from sun-ripened ingredients to recipes passed down through families.

You'll find taverns spilling out onto cobbled streets, their tables covered with crisp white cloths and the scent of grilled meats or fresh herbs drifting in the breeze. Start with local staples like moussaka, pastitsada, or rabbit stifado. These dishes are rich, satisfying, and layered with spices and slow-cooked flavors that make them truly unforgettable.

Must-Try Zakynthian Dishes

1. Rabbit Stifado

This hearty stew is a staple of Zakynthian home cooking. Rabbit is slowly braised in a rich sauce of tomatoes, onions, wine, garlic, and aromatic spices until the meat is fall-off-the-bone tender. It's deeply savory with just a hint of sweetness from the caramelized onions. You'll find excellent versions in traditional mountain tavernas such as *Porto Limnionas Tavern* or *Taverna To Petrino* in the village of Agios Leon. A generous portion typically costs around €13–€15. It's a satisfying and robust dish, perfect for dinner with a glass of local red wine.

2. Ladotyri Zakynthou (Zakynthian Olive Oil Cheese)

This unique cheese is made from sheep or goat milk and aged in olive oil, giving it a bold, tangy flavor with a salty edge. It's slightly crumbly and often served grilled or alongside fresh bread and olives. You can try it at *Paraga Taverna* in Alykes or buy it fresh from *Aristeon Olive Press* in Lithakia, which also offers cheese tastings. A small tasting portion in a restaurant costs about €6, while a block for takeaway is around €8–€10. It's not sweet at all; this is a sharp, savory treat.

3. Pastitsio

Often described as Greek lasagna, pastitsio is a comforting baked dish made with layers of tubular pasta, seasoned minced meat (often beef or lamb), and creamy béchamel sauce. The Zakynthian version tends to be spicier and richer than mainland styles. You'll find it in many family-run tavernas such as *Taverna Akrotiri* near Bochali. A portion costs between €9 and €11. It's savory with mild nutmeg sweetness in the béchamel, offering a well-balanced bite.

4. Bourdeto

A bold fish stew with Venetian roots, bourdeto is made with fresh scorpionfish or grouper cooked in a fiery tomato and red pepper sauce. It's intense, flavorful, and slightly spicy. The best place to enjoy it is at *Avli Taverna* in Zakynthos Town, which uses freshly caught fish from the nearby port. Expect to pay around €14–€18 depending on the fish. This dish is all about spice and depth, definitely not a sweet option.

5. Mandolato
This traditional Zakynthian nougat is made from honey, almonds, and egg whites, producing a chewy, airy texture with sweet, nutty flavors. It's a popular souvenir and a must-try for anyone with a sweet tooth. You'll find authentic mandolato at *Rakomelo Sweets Shop* or at the *Zante Traditional Sweets* stand in Zakynthos Town. A bar typically costs €2–€4. It's a delightful treat, especially with a cup of Greek coffee or a scoop of vanilla ice cream.

6. Skordostoumbi
This garlic-lovers' dream dish consists of eggplants stewed in a tangy tomato-garlic sauce and often served with fresh bread or potatoes. It has a slightly sweet undertone from slow-cooked tomatoes and is best enjoyed at vegetarian-friendly spots like *Votsalo* in Vasilikos. A main portion costs around €9. The dish strikes a lovely balance between savory and naturally sweet without being overpowering.

7. Zakynthian Souvlaki
This island twist on Greece's famous grilled skewers features pork or chicken marinated with olive oil, lemon, and local herbs, then grilled and served in warm pita with salad and tzatziki. Try it from street vendors in Zakynthos Town or beachside eateries like *Michaelos Grill House* in Kalamaki. It's both affordable and filling, usually costing €3.50–€5 per wrap. It's savory, fresh, and a must for lunch on the go.

Best Tavernas & Seafront Dining in Zakynthos

1. Porto Limnionas Tavern – Porto Limnionas

Perched above the dramatic cliffs of Porto Limnionas, this family-run taverna offers unforgettable views and equally unforgettable food. Known for its grilled octopus, stuffed vegetables, and fresh seafood platters, the menu is rooted in rustic Zakynthian flavors with a modern touch. Expect a meal for two with wine to cost around €40–€50. Most dishes here are savory, herb-forward, and Mediterranean in spirit, though you can round out your meal with a spoonful of homemade Greek yogurt topped with local honey for a mildly sweet finish.

2. Taverna Votsalo – Vasilikos

Set in the tranquil village of Vasilikos, Taverna Votsalo is ideal for those looking for traditional Greek cooking just steps from the sea. Their moussaka is particularly well-regarded, and their slow-cooked lamb with lemon potatoes is a standout. You'll dine under a canopy of olive trees with the sound of the waves nearby. Prices are reasonable, with mains ranging from €10 to €14. The cuisine leans heavily on savory and earthy notes, though their walnut cake with syrup offers a rich, sticky-sweet dessert for those looking to indulge.

3. The Garden – Tsilivi

This charming open-air restaurant lives up to its name with lush greenery surrounding a beautifully lit garden dining space. The menu is creative without losing touch with local roots, think sea bass baked in parchment, zucchini fritters, and feta cheese wrapped in phyllo and drizzled with honey. Located in Tsilivi, The Garden is perfect for a relaxed dinner with friends or a romantic night out. Main dishes average around €15, and the dessert options include both fruit-forward and honey-based sweets.

4. Taverna Xigia – Xigia Beach

Overlooking the mineral-rich Xigia Beach, this humble taverna feels like a hidden gem. It's known for its grilled sardines, feta-stuffed peppers, and excellent house wine served in traditional copper jugs. The setting is informal and authentic, with a few tables offering direct views of the sparkling Ionian Sea. A meal here costs around €12–€20 per person. The menu is largely savory, with fresh ingredients that highlight the island's coastal bounty, but they do serve a classic orange cake for those wanting a sugar-kissed ending.

5. Avli Taverna – Zakynthos Town

Located in the heart of Zakynthos Town but tucked away from the main streets, Avli offers a peaceful courtyard setting with soft lighting and a slow, welcoming pace. Their standout dishes include bourdeto (spicy fish stew), Zakynthian-style pastitsio, and wild greens pie. It's a great place to sample authentic flavors without the touristy atmosphere.

A full meal here costs about €25–€30 per person including wine. Their desserts, such as mandolato or semolina halva, lean more toward nutty and subtly sweet profiles.

6. Prosilio – Zakynthos Town

For a more upscale dining experience, Prosilio blends contemporary Greek cuisine with high-end presentation. Dishes like black truffle risotto, grilled tuna with fava purée, and deconstructed Greek salad reflect the chef's creative approach. Located near the central square in Zakynthos Town, the restaurant features a sleek indoor space and quiet outdoor terrace. Expect to spend around €60–€80 for two with drinks. Their dessert list includes sophisticated takes on traditional sweets, such as mastiha panna cotta or chocolate baklava beautifully balanced and not overly sugary.

7. El Sueño – Laganas Beach

This beachside restaurant is best known for its unbeatable sunset views and Mediterranean fusion dishes. Think seafood linguine, grilled prawns with ouzo sauce, and refreshing watermelon-feta salads. It's a stylish yet laid-back spot ideal for a long, leisurely dinner just steps from the sea. Prices range from €15–€20 per entrée. For dessert, their lemon tart and berry cheesecake provide a bright, mildly sweet ending to a savory meal.

Vegetarian & Vegan Options in Zakynthos

1. Essence Restaurant – Kalamaki

Essence is one of Zakynthos' most well-regarded spots for upscale vegetarian and vegan cuisine. Tucked away in Kalamaki, this elegant garden-style restaurant puts a creative twist on Greek and Mediterranean dishes. Their vegan moussaka, made with layers of eggplant, zucchini, and lentils topped with almond milk béchamel, is a must-try. The jackfruit souvlaki and grilled tofu skewers are also standout options. Main dishes range from €14 to €18. While most plates are savory, desserts such as coconut panna cotta and vegan chocolate mousse provide a satisfying but not overly sweet finale.

2. Cool Peppers Beach Bar & Restaurant – Laganas

Though Cool Peppers caters to a wide variety of tastes, their vegan and vegetarian menu has become a highlight. Located right on the sand in Laganas, this beachfront eatery offers a chilled-out atmosphere with hearty veggie-friendly dishes like quinoa salads, falafel wraps, and grilled veggie burgers with sweet potato fries. A filling main costs between €10 and €15. Their vegan mango sorbet and chia pudding are naturally sweet and refreshing, ideal for cooling off after a day at the beach.

3. Avli Taverna – Zakynthos Town

This quaint courtyard taverna in Zakynthos Town does an excellent job of accommodating plant-based diners without sacrificing traditional flavor. Their spanakopita (spinach pie), briam (roasted vegetables in olive oil), and stuffed vine leaves are all vegetarian classics made with love. Vegan guests can request slight modifications with no fuss. Meals here are affordably priced, typically €8 to €12 per dish. Finish with a slice of orange cake or local fruit preserves for a light and sweet conclusion.

4. The Halfway House – Tsilivi

The Halfway House, found just off the main road in Tsilivi, features a thoughtful menu with clearly marked vegetarian and vegan dishes. Their roasted chickpea salad, stuffed zucchini flowers, and tomato fritters are full of flavor and generous in portion size. Prices for mains hover around €9 to €13. Sweet lovers can enjoy vegan baklava or the tangy lemon sorbet, which strikes a nice balance between refreshing and sweet without being heavy.

5. The Green Boat – Argassi

This casual eatery with outdoor seating has become a quiet favorite for those seeking affordable, healthy vegetarian meals. Located in the heart of Argassi, The Green Boat serves fresh smoothies, Buddha bowls, avocado toast, and a daily vegan special made with seasonal produce. Mains start as low as €7 and rarely exceed €12.

6. Natura Grill – Alykes

Though best known for its grilled meats, Natura Grill in Alykes surprises with a generous vegetarian section. Their grilled halloumi with honey, baked aubergine with tomato and herbs, and creamy fava purée offer bold flavors and satisfying textures. Most mains are under €10, making it a budget-friendly option for those exploring the northeast coast. The honey-sweetened yogurt with walnuts, while not vegan, is a favorite among vegetarians seeking a simple, naturally sweet end to their meal.

7. Pita Break – Zakynthos Town

For fast, filling, and affordable vegetarian eats, Pita Break in the heart of Zakynthos Town delivers. Their falafel wraps, veggie gyros, and grilled vegetable pitas are made fresh to order and can be customized for vegans. A meal here typically costs just €5 to €8. Their tahini-based halva and sesame bars offer a sweet, nutty snack option that aligns well with plant-based diets.

Beach Bars and Local Wines in Zakynthos

1. Barracuda Beach Bar – Alykes

Located right on the golden sands of Alykes, Barracuda Beach Bar is a go-to destination for relaxed daytime lounging and scenic sunset sipping. Their menu features local Zakynthian wines, including semi-sweet white varieties like Verdea and dry reds from regional vineyards. A glass costs around €5, and bottles range from €18 to €25. Pair your drink with light meze grilled halloumi, olives, or tomato bruschetta for a balanced experience that highlights the fresh, savory flavors of the Ionian.

2. Casa Playa – Laganas Beach

This chic and stylish beach bar in Laganas offers a more upscale twist, ideal for those who enjoy sipping wine with their toes in the sand. The wine list includes boutique Zakynthian labels and rare finds like the semi-dry Avgoustiatis, a red grape native to the island that brings a light, fruity sweetness. Wines by the glass are priced between €6 and €8, and a bottle can go up to €30. Their small plates and seafood platters are thoughtfully designed to complement the wine, with subtle herbs and citrus notes enhancing the tasting experience.

3. Porto Paradiso – Vasilikos

In the lush, green setting of Vasilikos, Porto Paradiso Beach Bar blends casual island charm with refined local flavor. They offer an impressive selection of Zakynthian wines, with a particular focus on dry whites and rosés that go beautifully with sea views and sunshine. Try the earthy and slightly sweet Robola, paired with grilled calamari or a citrus salad. Prices are moderate, with most wines available by the glass for €4 to €6. The beachside setting adds to the relaxed vibe, making it ideal for lingering over your drink.

4. Infinity Beach Club – Tsilivi

Infinity Beach Club is where laid-back meets stylish, perched along the shore in Tsilivi. Known for its cocktails and music, it also boasts a curated list of local wines from family-run vineyards around Zakynthos. Expect floral, lightly sweet whites and bold reds with subtle spice. Glasses are typically €5–€7, and bottles average €20–€28.

The club serves tapas-style plates like feta-stuffed peppers and zucchini fritters, which strike a savory balance with the wine and round out the experience without overpowering the palate.

5. Banana Baya – Banana Beach
Banana Baya offers a colorful, energetic atmosphere just steps from the sea. This beach bar highlights Zakynthos' younger wine producers, with crisp rosés and semi-sweet whites popular among sunbathers and locals alike. Pair a chilled glass of Verdea (around €5) with light snacks like melon and prosciutto or a fresh salad. The flavors lean toward the refreshing and mildly sweet, making them perfect for a summer afternoon beneath an umbrella.

6. Vardiola Beach Bar – Keri
Set near the edge of Keri's pebbled coastline, Vardiola Beach Bar is quiet, romantic, and ideal for those looking to relax with a local glass in hand. The wine menu focuses on small-batch Zakynthian wineries and organic selections, often featuring semi-sweet red blends and crisp whites with honeyed undertones. A glass starts at €4.50, and the food leans toward homemade-style simplicity, think local cheese, olives, and warm bread. It's the kind of spot that invites slow conversation and long, peaceful afternoons.

7. Ammos Beach Club – Kalamaki
At Ammos in Kalamaki, the focus is on stylish comfort and local flavors. They carry several regional wines, including lesser-known varieties from the Ionian coast, many with fruity and slightly floral notes. Glasses are priced from €5 to €7, and the accompanying beach menu includes light grilled dishes, Mediterranean spreads, and seasonal fruit plates. The cuisine here is not overly sweet but occasionally complemented by sweet-savory elements like honey-drizzled cheese, enhancing the depth of the wines.

Traditional Sweets & Desserts in Zakynthos

1. Pasteli
Pasteli is a traditional Zakynthian sweet made from sesame seeds and local honey, often cut into thin bars or diamond-shaped pieces. It's delightfully crunchy with a deep, natural sweetness that isn't overwhelming. You can find high-quality pasteli at small bakeries and local shops like "Zakynthos Natural Products" in Zakynthos Town or at open-air markets. A small pack typically costs between €2 and €4. This treat travels well, making it a popular edible souvenir for visitors wanting to bring a bit of the island home.

2. Fitoura
Unique to Zakynthos, fitoura is a must-try semolina-based dessert served warm and dusted generously with cinnamon and sugar. It has a soft, creamy texture inside and a light crust outside, offering a sweet yet subtly spiced flavor.

Fitoura is commonly sold at street stalls and during local festivals, especially around Solomos Square. One portion costs about €2. It's often enjoyed as a quick snack while exploring town, and locals swear by its comforting, nostalgic flavor.

3. Mandolato

Mandolato is a traditional nougat made with egg whites, almonds, and honey or sugar syrup. It has a chewy texture and a pronounced sweetness, with toasted almonds adding a rich, nutty contrast. You can find it at shops like "To Paradosiako" near Bochali or at airport gift stores. Individual bars range from €2.50 to €5 depending on size and almond content. This dessert has roots in Venetian rule and remains a proud symbol of the island's culinary heritage.

4. Loukoumades

These golden, bite-sized doughnuts are deep-fried to perfection and typically served soaked in honey syrup with a sprinkle of cinnamon or crushed walnuts. They're crispy on the outside and pillowy inside, making them incredibly satisfying. You'll find loukoumades freshly prepared at traditional cafés in Zakynthos Town or seaside tavernas like "Taverna Zorbas" in Alykanas. A portion for sharing usually costs €4 to €6. Their sweetness comes mostly from the honey syrup, making them rich but not overpowering.

5. Amygdalota (Almond Biscuits)

Amygdalota are soft almond cookies, sometimes shaped into little crescents or round domes and dusted with powdered sugar. They have a delicate, marzipan-like sweetness and a rich almond aroma. These treats are often served at weddings and special occasions, but you can buy them year-round at bakeries such as "Katsarou Bakery" in Tsilivi. A small box costs around €5 to €7. They pair perfectly with a cup of Greek coffee or a glass of sweet dessert wine.

6. Diples

Diples are thin sheets of dough fried into crispy rolls or spirals and drizzled with honey and chopped walnuts. They're incredibly light, with a sweetness that comes entirely from the topping. Diples are usually made during holidays or celebrations but are also sold in local sweet shops like "Melissa Patisserie" in Zakynthos Town. A box of freshly prepared diples costs around €6 to €8. Their flaky texture and balanced flavor make them a favorite among both locals and visitors.

7. Spoon Sweets (Glyka tou Koutaliou)

These are fruits preserved in syrup and served by the spoonful, often accompanied by a glass of cold water. Common flavors include sour cherry, fig, and quince. Spoon sweets are intensely sweet, thanks to the syrup, but the natural flavor of the fruit still shines through. You'll find homemade versions at traditional tavernas and in local produce shops. A jar costs between €4 and €7 depending on the fruit. They're typically enjoyed as a light dessert or offered to guests as a gesture of hospitality.

Where to Stay in Zakynthos

Finding the right place to stay in Zakynthos really comes down to what kind of experience you're after. The island is incredibly diverse in its offerings: quiet hillside villages, lively beach resorts, charming harbor towns so choosing the right area can shape your whole trip.

Best Areas to Stay

Family-Friendly Stays

1. **Caretta Beach Hotel & Waterpark**
   Address: Kalamaki, Zakynthos
   Cost: from ~ €125/night (USD 137)
   Description: Offers a full waterpark experience, multiple pools, kids' club, and proximity to the beach all with buffet-style dining and active staff-led entertainment. Perfect for families looking for nonstop fun.

2. **Zante Pantheon Hotel**
   Address: Tsilivi, Zakynthos Town
   Cost: from ≈ $37/night
   Description: Budget-friendly but family-focused, with an outdoor pool, kid's pool, buffet breakfast, and cooking classes. Great value for families wanting convenience and comfort near Tsilivi Beach.

3. **Exotica Hotel & Spa by Zante Plaza**
   Address: Kalamaki Village, 29100 Kalamaki
   Cost: around €180/night
   Description: A four-star, family-oriented resort with spa, playground, pools, and babysitting. Quiet yet close to the beach ideal for families balancing relaxation and activity.

4. **Domes Aulūs Zante (Autograph Collection)**
   Address: Laganas Bay, 29100 Laganas
   Cost: mid–high range; all-inclusive
   Description: Stylish, all-inclusive resort on protected turtle nesting land, featuring multiple restaurants and bars, a kid's club, crèche, and spa perfect for a family treat with safety guarantees.

5. **Bay Hotel & Suites**
   Address: Zakynthos Town, near private sandy beach
   Cost: upscale (~€200+/night)
   Description: Five-star seafront resort with a private beach, spa, playground, tennis courts, and kid's club. Balances luxury with family needs—babysitting available for adults' romantic nights.

Romantic & Couples Escapes

1. **Olea All Suite Hotel**
   Address: Hill above Tsilivi
   Cost: from £240 (€280)/night
   Description: A stylish hideaway with olive grove views, plunge pools, spa, and a fine-dining restaurant. Ideal for romantic getaways with elegance and intimacy.

2. **King Jason Hotel**
   Address: Tsilivi hillside
   Cost: premium range
   Description: Adults-only boutique-style retreat with infinity pools, sea views, spa treatments, and wine tastings a peaceful, sophisticated haven for couples.

3. **Contessina Hotel**
   Address: 100 m from Planos beach, Tsilivi
   Cost: ~€150–€200/night
   Description: Adults-only with spa, chill vibe, and quiet location near the beach perfect for relaxing and recharging together.

4. **Villa at The Peligoni Club**
   Address: Northern Zakynthos (Agios Nikolaos)
   Cost: villas from £900/week + club membership (£375)
   Description: Luxurious coastal villas with access to beach club facilities, water sports, sunset dinners.

5. **Pierros Verde Resort**
   Address: Private beach north of Zakynthos Town
   Cost: mid to high range
   Description: Eco-chic, family-friendly resort with private beach and sophisticated rooms ideal for eco-conscious couples seeking understated luxury.

Adventure & Budget-Friendly Stays

1. **Ilaeira Rooms**
   Address: Argassi, 3 km from Zakynthos Town
   Cost: economical (~€60–€80/night)
   Description: Clean, modern rooms with kitchenettes, free Wi-Fi, and a short walk to the beach perfect for independent travelers and small groups on a budget.

2. **Callinica Hotel**
   Address: Tsilivi, near waterpark
   Cost: budget-mid (~€50–€90/night)
   Description: Basic apartments with shared pool, snack bar, and proximity to Tsilivi beach great for budget travellers wanting simple comforts.

3. **Jenny Hotel**
   Address: Agios Sostis, Laganas region
   Cost: budget-mid
   Description: Friendly, clean, with pool and playground, just 1 km from Laganas Beach ideal for adventure.

4. **Litore Luxury Living**
   Address: Laganas, 350 m from beach
   Cost: mid-range (~€120–€150/night)
   Description: Stylish and modern, with multiple pools and garden spaces great value for young couples and groups looking for comfort near the action.

5. **Varres Hotel**
   Address: Town hilltop, near Zakynthos Town
   Cost: mid (~€100–€150/night)
   Description: Quiet hillside retreat with pool, kid's pool, and views suitable for travellers valuing peace with occasional splashes of social atmosphere.

Countryside & Authentic Village Stays

1. **Lemon Garden Apartments**
   Address: Vasilikos, 700 m from Mavratzi Beach
   Cost: moderate (~€80–€120/night)
   Description: Sustainable traditional apartments with pool, mountain and sea views ideal for eco-minded travellers seeking peaceful countryside ambiance.

2. **Traditional Stone Villas via Peligoni Club**
   Address: Hills around Agios Nikolaos
   Cost: ~£900/week + club membership
   Description: Rustic luxury villas surrounded by olive groves, offering community and tranquility.

3. **Boutique Stone Mansion (unnamed)**
   Address: Fishing cove outside Town
   Cost: ~€140–€200/night
   Description: Converted stone manor with organic restaurant and cozy suites near cove perfect for those seeking authenticity in a boutique setting.

4. **Olea All Suite Hotel**
   Also fits here for countryside feel)

5. **Park Hotel & Spa**
   Address: Tsilivi area
   Cost: mid (~€100–€150/night)
   Description: Four-star with spa, pools, and quiet corner near the beach blends wellness with convenience for relaxed countryside stays.

Beachside & Activity-Focused Stays

1. **Poseidon Beach Hotel**
   Address: 500 m from Laganas centre
   Cost: ~€160–€200/night
   Description: Two pools (one for kids), playground, free beach sunbeds, and proximity to the main strip ideal for families or young travellers seeking beach access and fun.

2. **White Olive Premium Laganas**
   Address: 100 m from Laganas Beach
   Cost: ~€140–€180/night
   Description: Modern four-star with three pools and gym well-suited for couples or groups wanting comfort steps from the sand.

3. **Al Mare Hotel**
   Address: Beachfront, Tsilivi
   Cost: €80–€120/night
   Description: Bright sea-view rooms and suites, buffet breakfast, two pools, and kids' pool perfect for families and budget-conscious sun lovers.

4. **Contessina Hotel**
   (Also ideal for beachside escapes)

5. **Zakantha Beach Hotel**
   Address: Argassi
   Cost: mid-range
   Description: Four-star, beachfront with pool, bar, restaurant, and accessible rooms great for families or couples seeking straightforward seaside comfort.

Top Resorts & Luxury Hotels

Porto Zante Villas & Spa

Location: Tragaki, Zakynthos (private bay)
Cost: From approx. €3,500/night (Deluxe Villa), up to €20,000/night (Imperial Spa Villa)
Highlights: Ultra-luxe all-villa resort with private pools, boutique services (Armani furnishings, Bulgari toiletries), and butler service. Set in an intimate cliffside setting, this is a place for discreet, white-glove luxury.

Lesante Blu Exclusive Beach Resort (Adults Only)

Location: Tragaki, near Katragaki Beach
Cost: From £258 (€300)/night for B&B
Highlights: Adults-only oasis featuring ocean-view suites, infinity pools, spa facilities, and three dining venues (including fine-dining). Perfect for couples and honeymooners seeking serene, upscale relaxation.

Lesante Cape Resort & Villas

Location: Akrotiri village, secluded beach front
Cost: From £424 (€500)/night
Highlights: A Leading Hotels of the World property styled like a traditional Greek village. Offers villas with private pools, a high-end spa, on-site chapel, and folklore museum ideal for cultured luxury seekers.

Olea All Suite Hotel

Location: Hills above Tsilivi Beach
Cost: From £175 (~€200)/night
Highlights: A design-forward, adults-only retreat with 93 luxurious suites (many with private plunge pools), spa (with hammam and yoga pavilion), and a serene ambiance surrounded by olive groves.

Contessina Suites & Spa (Adults Only)

Location: Planos, Tsilivi (100 m from the beach)
Cost: From ~€250/night
Highlights: Five-star boutique hotel with spa, garden terraces, private pools, and concierge service. Elegant, peaceful setting tailored for romantic getaways or wellness retreats.

Budget-Friendly Accommodations

Asteri Studios & Apartments

Address: Kalamaki, Zakynthos (~650 m from Kalamaki Beach)
Cost: From approx. €21–€25/night (USD 22–29)
Description: Surrounded by colorful flowers, Asteri offers simple self-catering studios with a seasonal outdoor pool, snack bar, and bicycle rental. It's perfect for travelers who want independence and proximity to the beach without splurging.

Elena S Studios

Address: Kalamaki, Zakynthos (233 yd from town centre)
Cost: From approx. €22/night (USD 23–24)
Description: With a seasonal freshwater pool and poolside lounge, Elena S Studios offers clean, compact units and bike rentals. It's a straightforward, friendly choice for solo travelers or couples seeking value close to Kalamaki's center.

Athina Apartments

Address: Kalamaki, 400 m from Kalamaki Beach
Cost: From around €26/night (USD 28–30)
Description: A family-run complex with landscaped gardens, Athina Apartment seats you close to the sand. Each unit features kitchen facilities, making it ideal for travelers who prefer cooking their own meals.

Merlis Studios

Address: Kalamaki Main Road
Cost: From approx. £52 (~€60)/night (USD 65)
Description: This family-run property offers well-equipped kitchenettes, balconies or terraces overlooking gardens, and a peaceful atmosphere just a short walk from Kalamaki Beach, an excellent pick for travelers wanting tranquility and self-catering convenience.

Sofia's Hotel

Address: Kalamaki, Zakynthos
Cost: From around £24–£28 (~€28–€33)/night (USD 37–40)
Description: Located in a lush garden setting a few minutes' walk from the beach, Sofia's offers comfortable rooms, an outdoor pool, and a laid-back, welcoming atmosphere ideal for guests after simple comforts and great value.

Booking Tips:

- Prices are based on summer rates (June–August); off-season rates may be lower.
- Rooms typically include kitchenettes or basic cooking facilities great for saving on meals.
- Most are within a 5–10 minute walk of Kalamaki Beach, with grocery shops and tavernas nearby.

Family-Oriented Lodging

Caretta Beach Hotel & Waterpark
Address: Kalamaki, Zakynthos 29100
Cost: From ~€120/night (~US $137)
Highlights: A perfect family base boasting six adult slides, six kid slides, a wave pool, lazy river, plus multiple pools and a kids' playground. There's a buffet restaurant, pool bar, and 24-hour front desk. Located just 800 meters from Kalamaki Beach, it is ideal for families wanting entertainment and beach access in one spot.

Marelen Hotel Zakynthos
Address: Box 6, Kalamaki 29100
Cost: From ~€68/night
Highlights: Budget-friendly yet feature-packed. Guests love the diverse buffet breakfast, good restaurant, and standout kid's pool and splash area adjacent to the adult pool. Bicycle rentals, boat tours, and horseback riding available on-site. About a 5-minute walk to Kalamaki Beach is great for families seeking value and convenience.

Zante Pantheon Hotel
Address: Tsilivi, Zakynthos Town
Cost: ~US $147/night (€135)
Highlights: Modern apartments with balconies, an outdoor pool, kid's pool, and family cooking classes. A peaceful garden setting yet just steps from Tsilivi Beach and shops. Perfect for families wanting spacious rooms with the flexibility to self-cater.

Domes Aulūs Zante, Autograph Collection (All-Inclusive, Adults & Kids)
Address: Laganas, Zakynthos 29100
Cost: From ~US $200+/night
Highlights: Family-friendly offshoot of an adults-only brand. Offers spacious family rooms, multiple pools (including a Family Zone), kids' club, playground, and babysitting services. Located on the sea turtle–protected coastline, it's all-inclusive with child- and parent-friendly activities and dining.

The Peligoni Club (Villa + Beach Club Package)
Address: Northern Zakynthos, near Agios Nikolaos
Cost: Villas from £908/week (€1,100); club membership from £375/adult, £250/child
Highlights: More than a hotel upmarket villa rentals with full access to a family-friendly beach club. Kids' programmes, crèche, water sports, fitness classes, and sociable evenings in clubs and restaurants. A true family community with Brits and Irish staff making it welcoming for all ages.

What Families Love:

- **Waterparks & Splash Zones:** Found at Caretta and Marelen.

- **Kid-Focused Activities:** Available at Pantheon (classes), Domes (club), and Peligoni (events).

- **Beach Access:** All four are within walking distance—while Peligoni offers private beach club space.

- **Value & Convenience:** Buffet meals, self-catering apartments, pools, and on-site entertainment.

- **Variety:** From all-inclusive resorts to villa-plus-club experiences, there's something to match different family moods and budgets.

Romantic Getaways & Villas

Porto Zante Villas & Spa

Address: Tragaki, Zakynthos (private bay)
Cost: From approx. €3,000–4,500/night (Deluxe to Deluxe Spa Villa); Imperial Villa up to €20k
Description: An ultra-private, nine-villa enclave offering Butler service, heated pools, private beach access, Armani furnishings, and Bulgari toiletries. This sanctuary is designed for couples seeking impeccable service and absolute serenity, the kind of place where time slows and every detail pampers your soul.

Lesante Blu Exclusive Beach Resort *(Adults Only)*

Address: Tragaki, near Katragaki Beach
Cost: From £258 (€300)/night B&B
Description: A serene adults-only retreat set between olive groves and the sea, featuring ocean-view suites, infinity pools, a spa, and three dining venues. Ideal for romantic escapes luxury without haste, where sunset dinners become memories.

Lesante Cape Resort & Villas

Address: Akrotiri village, beachfront
Cost: From £424 (€500)/night
Description: A Leading Hotels of the World property styled like a traditional Ionian village. Offers private pool villas, spa, chapel, and folklore museum.

Olea All Suite Hotel *(Adults Only)*

Address: Hills above Tsilivi Beach
Cost: From £175 (€200)/night
Description: A design-forward sanctuary of 93 stylish suites, many with private plunge pools and outdoor terraces. Surrounded by olive groves, the hotel includes a spa, hammam, yoga pavilion, and refined dining ideal for couples who love purposeful calm and elegant simplicity.

Contessina Suites & Spa *(Adults Only)*

Address: Planos, Tsilivi (100 m from beach)
Cost: From ~€250/night
Description: Intimate and elegant, this boutique five-star offers garden terraces, private pools in select suites, a serene spa, and hip yet sophisticated decor.

Agritourism & Village Stays

Ktima Kourou (Tragaki)

Address: Tragákion, 29100 Tragaki
Cost: From ~ €1425/night
Description: A beautifully restored stone-built countryside estate set on a lush 6,000 m² olive grove. With free Wi-Fi, garden terraces, and peaceful stone cottages, it's ideal for travelers looking to unplug in rustic luxury complete with serene mornings and olive tree-dappled evenings.

Logothetis Organic Farm (Vasilikos)

Address: Vasilikos peninsula
Cost: Typically ~ €120–270/night (villa style)
Description: A working organic olive farm that welcomes visitors to stay in traditional countryside villas. Bike rentals help you explore the groves; olive oil tastings, farm tours, and horseback rides make it a lively yet peaceful family or couple-friendly retreat.

Alkis Farm & Residence (Gyri)

Address: Gyri, Zakynthos
Cost: Varies by unit typically €100–350/night
Description: Set amid vineyards and open fields, Alkis offers self-catered units in a charming rustic setting. It features peaceful gardens, a pool, and family-friendly amenities like playgrounds and bikes. Ideal for travelers who enjoy gentle rural exploration with handy comforts.

Agro Art Boutique Villa (Vanáton)

Address: Vanáton, eastern Zakynthos
Cost: From ~ €200–€300+/night (villa)
Description: A striking blend of modern comfort and local vernacular architecture with hot tub, sauna, two pools, on-site playground, and barbecue terraces. Perfect for couples or families wanting privacy, countryside scenery, and a touch of design flair.

Practical Travel Tips for Zakynthos

Driving in Zakynthos (Rentals, Rules, Parking)

Getting around Zakynthos is relatively simple, especially with a rental car or scooter. You'll find car rental agencies at the airport, in Zakynthos Town, and in all major resorts like Laganas, Tsilivi, and Kalamaki. Prices typically start around €30 per day for a compact car in low season, increasing during the busy summer months. EU and UK drivers can use their home license, but others might need an international permit. Drive on the right-hand side and always wear seatbelts. Local roads can be narrow, especially in mountain villages, so take your time. Parking in town centers may be tight, but beach areas and resorts usually offer ample space. Just avoid leaving valuables in your vehicle, especially near isolated viewpoints or beaches.

Emergency Contacts

In case of an emergency, dial 112 the Europe-wide emergency number. For police assistance, 100 connects you directly to law enforcement, while 166 is the number for ambulance services. The fire brigade can be reached at 199. English is generally spoken well enough for basic communication, especially in tourist areas. It's also a good idea to have your hotel or rental contact saved in case you need local help quickly.

Health & Medical Facilities

Zakynthos has a public hospital located just outside Zakynthos Town, offering 24/7 emergency care. There are also several private clinics around the island, particularly in tourist areas like Laganas and Tsilivi. Pharmacies are easy to spot and look for a green cross and pharmacists are well-trained, often offering solid advice for minor health issues. Most clinics accept travel insurance, but it's smart to carry your EHIC or GHIC card (for EU and UK citizens) or proof of coverage to avoid extra costs.

Accessibility Tips

Zakynthos is gradually improving in terms of accessibility, but not all areas are equally equipped. Resorts like Tsilivi and Kalamaki are more wheelchair-friendly with flatter terrain, accessible restaurants, and hotels that offer adapted rooms. Some of the main beaches, such as Kalamaki and Alykes, have ramps or wooden walkways for easier access. If you plan to rent a car, check with the agency in advance for availability of vehicles with automatic transmission or hand controls.

Travel Apps & Tools for Zakynthos

Before your trip, downloading a few apps can make your stay smoother. "Google Maps" is reliable for navigation around the island, and "Zakynthos Travel Guide" or "Visit Greece" apps can give you up-to-date info on attractions and events.

For car rentals, apps like DiscoverCars or Rentalcars help compare prices. Local taxis can be ordered via phone more often than app, but "Taxiplon" may work in Zakynthos Town. Offline translation apps like Google Translate also come in handy if you venture into less touristy spots.

What to Pack
Pack light, breathable clothing for the summer like cotton shirts, shorts, sundresses, and swimwear. A sunhat and strong sunscreen are essential, especially between June and August. Sturdy sandals or walking shoes are useful for exploring trails or rocky beaches. In spring and early fall, throw in a light jacket or sweater for the evenings. Don't forget mosquito repellent and a small first-aid kit. If you plan on visiting churches or monasteries, bring something modest to cover shoulders or knees out of respect for local customs.

Glossary & Greek Phrases

Essential Words for Travelers
Getting by in Zakynthos is easy with a warm smile and a handful of Greek words. While most locals in tourist areas speak English, dropping a "Kalimera" (good morning) or "Efharistó" (thank you) adds charm to any interaction. Start with basics like "Geia sou" (hello), "Parakaló" (please/you're welcome), "Signómi" (sorry/excuse me), and "Poso kostízei?" (how much does it cost?).

For restaurant visits, knowing "Neró" (water), "Psári" (fish), and "Krasi" (wine) can help you navigate menus more confidently. Even a simple "To logariasmó, parakaló" (the bill, please) is appreciated when dining out.

Common Signs and Phrases
On the road, you might spot signs like "Exodos" (exit), "Eísodos" (entrance), "Stási" (bus stop), or "Prosochí" (caution). In public areas, "Andres" and "Gynaíkes" mean men and women useful for bathroom signs. You'll often hear "Kalos írthate" (welcome), especially in hotels, and "Kalo taxídi" (have a good trip) when leaving. If someone asks "Miláte Angliká?" they're wondering if you speak English. Saying "Den katalavaíno" (I don't understand) is a polite way to express confusion, and locals will usually do their best to help.

Pronunciation Guide
Greek might look tricky at first glance, but it's more phonetic than it seems. Most letters are pronounced as they appear. The letter "G" as in "Efharistó" sounds like a soft "H," and "Kalimera" is pronounced "kah-lee-MEH-rah." "Geia sou" is said like "yah soo," and "Krasi" is "krah-SEE." The key is to stress the right syllable; it often falls on the second or third. Practice slowly and listen closely to how locals say things. Even if your accent's off, most people will appreciate the effort and respond with a smile.

One More Look

As your Zakynthos journey winds to a close, the memories you've gathered will begin to take root not just in your camera roll, but in your senses and your spirit. You'll remember the cool, salty breeze brushing against your face as your boat rounded the cliffs of Navagio. You'll think back to the golden afternoons spent sipping local wine at a beachside taverna, and the sound of traditional music drifting through the night air in a quiet village square. This isn't just a destination, it's a living postcard, painted in brilliant blues and lush greens, with every corner offering something charming, heartfelt, and utterly unforgettable.

Zakynthos has a way of slowing you down, inviting you to breathe deeply, eat well, laugh often, and connect with the island's warm-hearted soul. From its dramatic coastlines to its olive-scented countryside, its rich heritage to its fresh, flavorful cuisine, every moment here feels like a reward for choosing adventure over routine, and wonder over the familiar.

So as you prepare to leave, don't be surprised if you already find yourself planning your return. Zakynthos has that effect. It stays with you in stories, in flavors, and in that sweet sense of joy you only get from discovering somewhere that truly feels like a hidden part of you. Your journey may be ending for now, but the island's magic is just beginning to unfold.

Printed in Dunstable, United Kingdom